Jc

OF A FOLLOWER
OF ST. BENEDICT

An Exploration of Joy in Lent
and in the Whole of Christian Life

JOY IN THE LIFE OF A FOLLOWER OF ST. BENEDICT

An Exploration of Joy in Lent and in the Whole of Christian Life

Fr. Donald S. Raila, O.S.B.

Reidhead & Company Publishers
Bishop, California

ISBN 978-1-940777-94-8

Imprimi Potest:
Rt. Rev. Martin R. Bartel, O.S.B.
Archabbot, Saint Vincent Archabbey

Nihil Obstat:
The Reverend Monsignor Raymond E. Riffle MSW, MPA, VG
Censor Liborum

Imprimatur:
The Most Reverend Larry J. Kulick, JCL
Bishop of Greensburg
Date: March 19, 2022

*The nihil obstat and imprimatur are official declarations that a book or pamphlet is free of
doctrinal or moral error. No implication is contained therin that those who have granted the
nihil obstat and imprimatur agree with the contents, opinions or statement expressed.*

Reidhead & Company Publishers
www.reidheadpublishers.com
Bishop, California

This book is set in Minion Pro, designed by Robert Slimbach for Adobe Systems.
It was inspired by the elegant and highly readable typefaces of the late Renaissance.

I would like to dedicate this book to my deceased parents, grandparents, and godparents, who helped me to learn the value of sacrifice and perseverance in order to attain a greater good. That preparation helped me to realize later that the perseverance through difficulties, in the Christian sense, is a profoundly meaningful share in the Cross of Christ and that the ultimate greater good consists of the anticipatory joy of conformity with Christ on this earth and then the fullness of joy in heaven in communion with the Blessed Trinity and all the saints.

Contents

FOREWORD

Father Donald Raila's reflections on *Joy in the Life of a Follower of Saint Benedict* address not a single situation or even multiple situations that we encounter in life. Rather, they focus on the attitude with which the follower of Saint Benedict confronts the various challenges that he or she faces. Sometimes joy will be a natural reaction to the gift of grace, and at other times it will call one to deeper reflection before the cause for joy can be really understood.

The initial impulse for his book goes back to a retreat conference that the young Abbot Giuseppe Nardin, O.S.B., Abbot of Saint Paul Outside-the-Walls, gave to the community at the Benedictine College of Sant'Anselmo in Rome during Lent of 1980. In his conference Abbot Nardin mentioned that Saint Benedict speaks of joy only twice in the *Holy Rule*, and both times in Chapter 49: "On the Observance of Lent." I remember walking in the garden at Sant'Anselmo after the conference and reflecting on what I considered to be an interesting, if not strange, phenomenon: writing about joy only in the context of Lenten observance.

As time and other commitments permitted, I was able to defend my doctoral dissertation, which had been written under the direction of Father Adalbert de Vogüé, in November of 1993 with the title *Joy in Lent: Gaudium in Chapter 49 of the Regula Benedicti: The Monastic and Liturgical Contexts.*

My confrere Fr. Donald was interested and read the dissertation, and as the reader of this book will see, he took it beyond the confines of an academic dissertation and showed how the theme of Christian joy permeates the whole life of a disciple of Christ and of Saint Benedict. Reflecting as he does on joy in the sacred liturgy and in the teachings of Julian of Norwich, St. Teresa of Calcutta, Fr. Jacques Philippe, St. Paul VI, St. John Paul II, Pope-emeritus Benedict XVI, and Pope Francis, Fr. Donald provides numerous examples of how joy is, or at least should be, found throughout one's Christian life, all the while weaving this fabric into his own Christian and monastic journey.

Although this book does not address itself directly to a culture that is largely lacking in joy, an entertainment culture and a culture that reveals within itself a deep inner emptiness, Fr. Donald does name these challenges and notes that our society's craving for earthly satisfaction does not lead to joy; rather, only union with God makes one joyful. Fr. Donald distinguishes joy from physical or emotional pleasure and points out the vanity of these pleasures when sought for themselves, the vanity resulting from the fact that our desires can fluctuate greatly and our sources of pleasure can easily change over time. In contrast, Fr. Donald sees joy as a characteristic of the fruit of the Spirit and true Christian joy as something supernatural. It always has to do with union with God and living attached to the good, the true, and the beautiful - even when such living involves sacrificing for the other person, and especially for the Other, who is God Himself.

If, as Saint Benedict writes in his chapter on the observance of Lent, the life of a monk ought always to have the character of a Lenten observance, then the attitude of joy, a characteristic of the fruit of the Spirit, obliges the follower of Saint Benedict at all times. In other words, a true follower of Saint Benedict, like every committed Christian, lives in joy and does all things with joy. Thanks be to God.

Fr. Kurt Belsole, O.S.B.

INTRODUCTION

On Joy in Christian Life

During leisurely vacation time in August 1996, I recalled an experience of joy that had attracted me to Fr. Kurt Belsole's dissertation many months before. Occasions of joy stimulated my interest in taking up this project of reflecting on Christian joy, especially as presented in the *Holy Rule* of St. Benedict. Then on a weekend, as I celebrated Masses in my home parish, I saw in the opening prayer a marvelous contrast between Christian joy and peace and the passing attractions of this world.

The alternative opening prayer in the 1970 *Sacramentary* for the Twenty-first Sunday in Ordinary Time read:

> Lord God, give your people the joy of hearing your word
> in every sound and of longing for your presence more
> than for life itself. May all the attractions of a changing
> world serve only to bring us the peace of your kingdom,
> which this world does not give.

Yes, I thought, true joy involves hearing God's loving word in every experience and longing to respond fully to His redeeming presence. This hearing and longing bring us joy even if they lead to the loss of our very earthly lives. They bring about a sort of "death to self" insofar as we must leave behind our self-centered attachments to make more room for God in our lives.

After Mass on that Sunday morning, the sacristan and I began to share about the day's Gospel. He reminded me that it is we who must adjust ourselves to what God teaches through the Church and that we can find ultimate satisfaction only from such obedience to His mysterious ways. This conversation led me to consider a page from Saint Mother Teresa's book *Total Surrender*, which I had been using for my spiritual reading:

> The more repugnant the work, the greater should be our faith and cheerful devotion. That we feel repugnance is but natural, but when we overcome it for love of Jesus we may become heroic. Very often it has happened in the lives of the saints that a heroic overcoming of repugnance has been what has lifted them to sanctity" (*TS*, p. 30).

Yes, true joy comes from doing even "naturally repulsive" things because it is then that we know our need for God's grace; it is only His grace that enables us to do the difficult thing and to do it cheerfully. Perhaps, then, there is even greater Christian joy in experiences that are seemingly undesirable than in those which are naturally attractive; for in the former we know that we can endure and even be cheerful only because of God's grace, which redeems us from despairing, murmuring, or giving up on a task which He has given us.

The next morning the pastor and I were reflecting on the same opening prayer. When I mentioned my enthusiasm over the dissertation *Joy in Lent*, he responded with the happy assertion that he had written a dissertation, perhaps some 50 years earlier, on the occurrence of "consolation" in the works of Pope St. Gregory the

Great. In his research, he had discovered that Christian consolation, like joy, often manifests itself amid crosses. How true it was! Here was another wonderful reminder that Christian joy comes as an ever-available gift, no matter what we may feel or think in response to external circumstances. We can rejoice that our God of joy and peace is ever-present to redeem us. He redeems us not only from sin and death but, very practically, from our fears of not finding anything good in a particular situation. All these experiences gave me the zeal and joy to keep reading, reflecting, and writing about the marvelous gift of joy that Our Lord holds out to us at all times.

After these initial experiences, work on this project came to a halt, except for a few efforts over the years. Then in March 2020, the coronavirus pandemic struck the world, and the quarantine provided an opening for me to resume work on this book—twenty-four years later. I finally had the time, energy, and motivation to continue and, I hope, to complete this project.

Is there anything joyful about this pandemic? Certainly on the surface there is nothing to rejoice about a worldwide health threat, millions of deaths, innumerable illnesses, billions of hours of lost work, enormous harm done to countries' economies, the massive closing of educational institutions and businesses, or people's feelings of depression and discouragement. Amid all this disruption, however, we may be able to discern some blessings. Here at Saint Vincent Archabbey, some of the monks have had to slow down because of the cancellation of public Masses, "weekend missions," meetings, trips for various purposes, and other time-consuming endeavors. Some of us have had more time to catch up on postponed projects. There is a sense of solidarity in our community through bearing with restrictions imposed by the virus and deciding on our communal response to the virus. We are also being challenged to trust in God more radically since we do not know from day to day what further changes the next day will bring.

Ironically, all this began during the Season of Lent, when all of us Christians are called to participate with special intensity in the suffering and death of Christ our Lord. Like the crucifixion of Christ and its fulfillment in the Resurrection, perhaps this coronavirus is opening the world and the Church to a great outpouring of grace. It may even move some unbelievers to turn to God, to rely on His mercy, and to practice His love in their lives. Crises can help people to reorder their priorities and to see more clearly what is really important. We can pray that this crisis will provide us all with a wake-up call to recognize the wonderful truth of the Father's plan for the world in Christ and to cooperate with that plan with greater zeal. Even a partial fulfillment of that prayer would truly be a cause for joy!

This joy is also akin to the blessedness promised in the Beatitudes, in which Our Lord promises fullness of life to those who would be naturally unhappy according to this world's standards. The fact that such blessed people have come to know God in their emptiness and poverty opens them to hope for full blessedness in the future and to experience joyful anticipations of blessedness even in this "valley of tears." In his book *The Eight Doors of the Kingdom: Meditations on the Beatitudes*, Fr. Jacques Philippe asserts that poverty of spirit, the subject of the first Beatitude, sums up all the other situations of blessedness. In reflecting on poverty of spirit, he quotes St. Thérèse of Lisieux, who found joy in her littleness and emptiness and whom he sees as a model of spiritual poverty. Fr. Philippe comments:

> Here we see Thérèse's wonderful equilibrium: great generosity and fidelity even in little things, but a confidence that always rests only on God and not on her own works. Always we are God's debtors, not with anguished guilt but

in trust and filial joy, glad to be sustained by him and not by our own efforts. We are happy to owe him everything because we make no pretense of self-sufficiency and are like little children, content to receive everything from the generous hand of our Father and to depend entirely on him for everything. Poverty is happiness because it makes us totally dependent on God and more completely attaches us to him. The goal of life is not to glorify ourselves or be satisfied with ourselves, but to glorify the infinite mercy of God to whom we owe everything (*EDK*, pp. 63-64). [Of course, here Fr. Philippe is not referring to material poverty or destitution, which Our Lord and the Church seek to eradicate from the earth.]

Countercultural though it may be, let us all seek the spiritual poverty that involves total trust in God, total dependence on God, and the glorification of God and not of ourselves. These attitudes will lead us to genuine and lasting joy, the same joy of which St. Benedict wishes us to partake most especially during Lent.

CHAPTER 1

Motivation to Explore the Notion of Christian Joy

We live in a culture that is largely lacking in joy. There is a great deal of frantic seeking after material pleasure, emotional stimulation, and intellectual gratification; these searches often arise from a deep inner emptiness. Furthermore, these quests lead to an even greater emptiness and to the sadness that comes from such emptiness. People joke about things that "have to" go wrong. People expect public officials to be corrupt. People live in fear of disasters which the media peddles and highlights. People live in fear even of minor losses because of a mindset that regards a loss as a threat to one's identity, as a sign of decreased control over life, and as a possible foreboding of future painful losses. Cynicism, depression, heaviness of heart, and chronic sadness abound because people cannot succeed in their relentless quest for happiness pursued in a self-centered, material way.

In contrast to this vain search, the Christian life is to be characterized by joy, as evidenced in the Scriptures and the teachings of the Church. The first three dimensions of the fruit of the Holy Spirit are love, joy, and peace (Gal 5:22-23), and these are very much related to one another. During the Last Supper, Jesus bequeathed a deep and abiding joy to His disciples. As He preached the commandment of love to them, He urged them to abide in His love, "that my joy may be yours and your joy may be complete" (John 15:11), and He prayed to the Father "that they may share my joy completely" (John 17:13). This was a joy that Our Lord apparently experienced even in his Passion and Death as He poured out His life in love and remained at peace because of His supreme trust in the Father. Many passages of the New Testament describe joy amidst trials. Furthermore, the *Rule of Saint Benedict*, in Chapter 49, entitled "The Observance of Lent," indicates that monks are to offer something extra to God "with the joy of the Holy Spirit" (*RB* 49:6) and to undertake practices of self-denial so that they might "look forward to holy Easter with joy and spiritual longing." (49:7). How can this be? How is it that monks and all Christians are to find joy in experiences of deprivation and of all sorts of suffering?

On April 17, 1994, Fr. Kurt Belsole, O.S.B., delivered a talk to Oblates of Saint Benedict gathered for a monthly meeting in Latrobe, Pennsylvania. As he enthusiastically shared excerpts from his doctoral dissertation *Joy in Lent*, I felt myself caught up in joyful appreciation of these remarks as describing something which lies at the very essence of Christian and monastic life. Joy in Lent, said Fr. Kurt, comes from "falling in love with God." When we love someone, he reminded us, it becomes a joy for us to sacrifice for the other person. Since trials offer the Christian an opportunity to surrender self-will and to trust in a loving God instead of in one's own agenda, why should difficulties <u>not</u> constitute special occasions of joy?

I emerged from Fr. Kurt's talk saddened only because it had not been recorded. I wondered, however, from reflection on my notes, if the fruits of his sharing could not be made available to Oblates in some other way. When I later had the privilege of reading Fr. Kurt's whole dissertation, I decided that it would be of great value for a broader audience to present in booklet the relevant excerpts from the dissertation along with reflections on Christian joy from other sources. Thus, over a period of some years and with the accumulation of more insights about joy from the liturgy and from other authors, this little book has taken shape. Through these groping observations, may the reader come to share in the joy of Christ in His total self-giving to the Father and to us. I believe this is the type of joy that Fr. Kurt radiated in his dissertation and his talk. It is also the type of joy that I strive to experience in my Christian, monastic journey—and in reflecting on Fr. Kurt's words and presenting them with a slightly different slant.

In the intervening twenty-six years, there has been an even greater need to offer Christian joy to a world entangled heavily in secularistic hopelessness and gloom. More and more I have discovered in various books of spiritual reading, perhaps as an antidote to this misery, an emphasis on joy as an essential element of the Christian (and human) journey on this earth and as a pointer to the ultimate joy that exists only in communion with God in eternity. More quotations on joy from other books will be offered in subsequent chapters of this book., but let me here give the following excerpt from Fr. Raniero Cantalamessa as one example of hope-filled literature of recent years that points to joy in Christian life. The author reflects in his book *Sober Intoxication of the Spirit, Part Two*:

> Since we can have an experience of eternity through faith, from now on we can also experience happiness [i.e., Christian joy]. Christians, like everyone else, want to be happy 'while we live in this flesh,' but we have discovered that there is another way to be happy. We have known the joy that is a 'fruit of the Spirit' and endures affliction, the joy that is not even here on earth a 'momentary' joy but a

profound and lasting peace. Paul could say, 'with all our affliction, I am overjoyed' (see 2 Corinthians 7:4b), and we read about the first disciples that they 'were filled with joy and with the Holy Spirit' (see Acts 13:52)" (*SISPT*, pp. 84-85).

May the Holy Scriptures, the *Rule* of Saint Benedict, and many contemporary Christian works lead us to appropriate the joy of the Holy Spirit that God desires for us so that we may hasten all the more zealously to the fullness of joy with all the angels and saints in the place in heaven that Christ has prepared for us (cf. Jn 14:2-3).

CHAPTER 2

A Definition of Christian Joy

Our secular world generally thinks of joy in a very limited and ultimately disappointing way. Joy is seen as the happiness that comes from having what one desires at any given moment, especially in terms of physical or emotional pleasure. However, as we know, such "joy" is fleeting because our desires can fluctuate greatly, and we rarely remain content with the present state of affairs. People with large amounts of money usually seek more and more. People with positions of influence usually crave even more power. People who delight in tasty food and depend on it for gratification will have an appetite for more and tastier food unless this desire is restrained by other desires that take into account one's long-range health and well-being. In these examples "joy" is not much different from "happiness," which depends so much on happenstance. If a situation happens to please me, I become happy, whereas if circumstances do not coincide with my particular liking, I become unhappy. Thus the quest for happiness results in a relentless and ultimately hopeless trajectory on a vicious circle since one's whimsical and ever-expanding desires can never be perfectly fulfilled. Despite the prevalent illusion that "just one more thing" or one more stimulating experience will bring true happiness, those who seek such earthly "joy" can only drive themselves to disappointment if not despair.

In contrast, Christian joy arises from possessing God or, at least, being on the way to possessing Him. In his dissertation Fr. Kurt writes:

> Anthropologically, and speaking in the broadest sense possible, joy can be described as the affective state of a person who is gladdened because he is in conscious possession of a good. In this broad sense, it is a synonym for 'pleasure.' In a more restricted sense, however, the term 'joy' can be reserved for that delight which is caused by spiritual goods. The human person can know joy only because he is a being of desire. That presupposes that he perceives outside of himself some good, real or imagined, to which he aspires. In a religious sense, however, more is implied. Because he is a spiritual being created by God and for God, the human person can never find rest, and, therefore, perfect joy other than in union with his Creator. This means that true calm, real peace, and the cessation of anxiety come with the delight of possessing the absolute good which is God [here there is a footnote with reference to St. Augustine's *Confessions*]. For Christians, this search for union with God becomes centered in the life and saving activity of Jesus Christ. We cannot unite ourselves to God unless he wills to give himself to us, i.e., we cannot receive joy except as a grace. This gift and this grace God has given to us in Jesus Christ. Joy in the mind of St. Paul is a fruit of the Holy Spirit (*Gal.* 5, 22), the Spirit sent by the resurrected Lord to his Church. Joy, then, is experienced in the life of the Christian who in faith, hope, and charity shares in the saving action of the cross of Christ" (*JL,* pp. 3-4).

In this sense joy is always available, whether one feels happy, sad, or neither particularly happy nor sad. Joy is a gift of God, but God is always making the gift available since the Father is always offering us divine life in Christ through the Holy Spirit. Although we are not yet in full possession of God, there is joy in our present degree of possessing God, and there is joy in the hope of possessing Him more fully. Even our experience of emptiness and loss provides an opportunity for Christian joy to emerge since that very lack is meant to be replenished by the fullness of God in Christ, who shares our neediness and uses it to draw us to Himself since He alone can make good of our deprivation. Our faith tells us that Christ came to save the sinner, that our very weaknesses can open us (if we choose) to God's never-failing strength, and that even our fear of being unloved can and should open us to the unconditional, all-faithful love of God. In Christ God loves us in our abysmal misery, and He loves others through us as long as we are willing to receive from Him this great privilege of serving others as His instrument. Is there any reason, then, why we should not have joy? Furthermore, should we not seek to grow in our capacity to be immersed in this joy?

CHAPTER 3

Joy in the *Rule* of St. Benedict.

F r. Kurt writes that his study concerns "joy, or *gaudium*, as it is presented by Saint Benedict in *RB* 49, 6-7. Saint Benedict speaks of joy only twice in the Rule. Both occurrences of *gaudium* are found in *RB* 49: *De quadragesimae obseruatione* [on the Observance of Lent]. The first one deals with offering some extra sacrifice freely 'with the joy of the Holy Spirit,' and the second refers to awaiting Holy Easter 'with the joy of spiritual desire'" (*JL*, p. 1). Fr. Kurt continues, "Lent, however, for Benedict is not just one season of the year out of many. He writes at the beginning of *RB* 49 that the life of a monk ought always to have the character of a Lenten observance about it, but few monks have such virtue. Benedict then goes on to outline his program for Lent: prayer with tears, reading, compunction, abstinence, special prayers, and the giving up of some idle talk and jesting. All this is to be done with joy, but how -- and why? Our examination of the place of joy in Lent in *RB* 49, however, is more than just an inquiry into the interpretation of a passage of the *RB*. In other words, it is not only a 'monastic' question. One must ask, first of all, what joy is for the human person and the Christian before he considers what joy in Lent might mean for a monk. The question of what Benedict means by offering something with the joy of the Holy Spirit during Lent or awaiting Easter with the joy of spiritual desire must be answered in light of what joy is in human and Christian life" (*JL*, pp. 2-3).

Although St. Benedict uses "joy" only twice, he refers to situations of joy or delight in various experiences of monastic life that are mentioned in the *Rule*. The sections of the *Rule* which mention these experiences "often serve as conclusions or 'high points' to which the various chapters or segments of the Rule have been moving. In these conclusions, one finds a certain spiritual blossoming even in this life" (*JL*, p. 35). Thus these passages of the *Rule* both help us to understand what real joy in monastic life is meant to be and also accentuate joy as an essential part of monastic life, to be experienced all year long and in every circumstance. These other references to dispositions such as delight occur largely in the Prologue of the *Rule* and in Chapters 4, 7, and 72, especially in the conclusions of these chapters. Fr. Kurt comments that although St. Benedict borrowed extensively from other sources, the sections "which depict joy and delight … are [largely] proper to Benedict. These parts of the Rule show a man full of *pathos*. The otherwise sober Roman, who rather reservedly legislates for the daily schedule, the structure of the divine office, the manner of admitting brethren, and the measure of food and drink, becomes ardent and warm. In these sections, Benedict is most himself, and with a certain *sobria ebrietas* [sober inebriation] he keeps pointing out the transformation which can take place in the monk who abandons himself to faith, conversion, [and] the life of the Spirit, and who has learned to prefer nothing at all to Christ" (*JL*, p. 36).

In the Rule of St. Benedict joy is very much linked with the virtues of conversion, of patience with others in their weakness, and of overall growth in Christ. How, specifically, do we find joy in the various elements of Benedictine spirituality? Fr. Kurt first explores joy in monastic observances, some of which are mentioned in three lists of good works in *RB* 49. He writes, "At first glance these works might not seem to be very attractive. Prayer with tears, *lectio*, special prayers, and compunction might be tolerable enough, but some monks could look upon the prospects of less sleep, less talking, and less joking as a bit more burdensome. One might ask where joy enters in here" (*JL*, p. 277-278).

Fr. Kurt continues, "The gospel itself is the first witness to joy in these circumstances. Jesus instructs his disciples that when they fast they should not be sad like the hypocrites, but rather wash their faces and comb their hair so that people may not see that they are fasting (*Mt.* 6, 16)" (*JL*, p. 278). Early monastic writings likewise emphasize that observances like fasting nurture a spirit of joy. Through fasting monks acquire freedom of soul and learn how the kingdom of God is not a matter of food and drink but of justice, peace, and joy in the Holy Spirit (cf. Rom 14:17). John Cassian, in teaching about the sadness which comes from God and which leads to repentance, shows how this very sadness contains within itself the fruits of the Holy Spirit, including joy. He provides examples of joy occurring in contrition by mentioning that even beginners in monastic life can be overcome with ineffable joy as they offer up prayers with tears and that one who recalls his sins can experience an indescribably refreshing joy, again along with tears. The gift of God's forgiveness, to which we open ourselves as soon as we are repentant, leads us to possess God and so causes us joy. In sum, it is a paradox of Christian life that those experiences and practices which might seem most repulsive from a worldly perspective are the ones that dispose us to the most joy from a Christian perspective.

A secular view of Lenten observances might regard them as obstacles to joy. Fr. Kurt comments, "The scriptural sources and monastic tradition which Benedict knew associate them, however, with joy. Fasting, abstinence, repentance, and prayer are seen by the tradition not as obstacles to joy, but as ways to enter into it. *RB* 49 is a text proper to Benedict, one which he does not take from the *RM* [the *Rule of the Master*, from which St. Benedict borrowed extensively], and here he locates *gaudium* [joy] in the midst of an asceticism which he really believes should be exercised at all times. This chapter of the *RB* is an invitation to joy, and it is especially addressed to the monk who chooses to enter more deeply into monastic life. This is similar to another text proper to Benedict, viz., verse 49 of the Prologue. There Benedict writes that as one advances in monastic life and faith he runs the way of God's commandments with an expanded heart and the unspeakable sweetness of love. Joy in Lent is all that much more accessible as one gives himself over to the observances which Saint Benedict outlines in *RB* 49. Again, the Prologue provides a parallel experience, viz., the heart expands and one runs the way of God's commandments with a love which is unspeakable so that sharing in the *sufferings* of Christ, the monk might also merit a share in His kingdom (*RB* Prol. 49-50)" (*JL*, pp. 279-280).

Secondly, Fr. Kurt observes that the *Rule* associates joy with a new interior freedom that comes with a radical following of Christ. *How* we do things, in addition to *what* we do, can nurture a growth in joy. Just as "joy" is used in the phrase "with joy" in *RB* 49, other forms of delight found in *RB* Prol 4, 5, 7, and 72 are associated with the <u>way</u> in which one goes about one's observances. Monks find true delight in running the way of God's commandments "with an expanded heart" (Prol: 49), in yearning for eternal life "with all spiritual desire" (4:46), in obeying "willingly" (5:16), in embracing suffering "with a quiet heart" (7:35), in going their way "rejoicing" after suffering difficult things (7:39), in practicing good zeal "with the most fervent love" (72:3), in nurturing the fear of God "in love" (72:9), and in loving their abbot "with a sincere and humble love." (72:9). In contrast, one goes backward and loses potential rewards if one obeys cringingly, sluggishly, half-heartedly, unwillingly, or with murmuring (cf. 5:14, 18). Thus joy accompanies an attitude which freely consents to the triumph of God's will over natural human inclinations and grows when such an attitude is nurtured. Fr Kurt comments that "a certain ideal of interior freedom, of joy, of peace and calm, and of generosity, therefore, emerges in the sections of the *RB* which are dealing with some of the same elements of the spiritual life as is *RB* 49. That does not mean that Benedict expects that the ideal is already attained in these areas, but he presents its realization as a definite possibility which his monks should strive for. It is not something that comes naturally, but it can become, by choice and by practice, the way that one does things, i.e., one begins to do the good *uelut naturaliter* ['as though naturally'] (cf. *RB* 7, 68). The attitudes which Benedict recommends to his monks seem to have an element of the unconscious about them. Nonetheless, they can be cultivated and developed, and Benedict says that they should be. The monk can choose to keep his heart constricted, or he can allow it to expand. …[B]y the Holy Spirit, the Lord can manifest how his servant is moved no longer by fear in general (*formido*) or by the fear of hell (*timor gehennae*). Rather, these can be replaced by the love of Christ (*amor Christi*) and delight in virtue (*delectation uirtutum*) (cf. *RB* 7, 68-69), which then become the driving forces within him. If this can happen, Benedict's suggestion in *RB* 49, 6 that his monks offer something extra to God with the joy of the Holy Spirit makes perfect sense" (*JL*, pp. 282-283).

Thirdly, Fr. Kurt shows how true Christian joy comes with making Christ the center of our lives in all things. In fact, "the place of Christ has a special significance in the passages of the Rule which have been examined in their relationship to *RB* 49" (*JL*, p. 284). For example, it

13

is love of Christ that makes ready obedience possible (*RB* 5:2). Monks learn to pray for their enemies in the love of Christ (*RB* 4:72). After one has ascended the steps of humility, it is the love of Christ rather than fear that motivates a Christian's life (*RB* 7:69). Most especially, good zeal involves preferring nothing whatever to Christ (*RB* 72:11).

Associating joy with a continual and repeated focus on Christ reminds us, too, that Christian joy is not just a spontaneous feeling but something which can be taught and which we can be told to accept. At first glance, one might think it is only "a rather strange or perhaps even ill personality which needs to be told to rejoice" (*JL*, p. 285); it may seem obvious that people "know whether they should be happy or sad" (*JL*, p. 285). "Yet," Fr. Kurt observes, "the scriptures provide sufficient examples of the Lord or the apostles telling people to rejoice. Jesus, in the beatitudes, instructs the crowd that when they are persecuted on his account, they should rejoice because their reward is great in heaven (*Mt.* 5, 12; *Lk.* 6, 23). Paul tells the Christians at Rome to rejoice in hope (*Rom.* 12, 12). The *Letter of James* tells the brothers that they should consider it pure joy when they are subjected to various trials because trials make for endurance (*Jas.* 1, 2), and *First Peter* 4, 13 encourages its recipients to rejoice in their share in the sufferings of Christ because when his glory is revealed, they will rejoice exultantly" (*JL*, p. 285).

Fr. Kurt continues, "These passages of sacred scripture all address the danger that in trial or difficulty one might lose sight of the goal. [The Christian] might need to be reminded to rejoice in persecution because in the future his reward will be great in heaven, or to rejoice in hope in the future, or to recognize that trials make for endurance, or to rejoice in suffering with Christ because thus he will rejoice with Him in glory" (*JL*, pp. 285-286).

Fr. Kurt also comments, "Benedict, too, might need to remind his monks of the final goal of the monastic life, which is the kingdom of heaven. In *RB* 49, it seems that he aims at encouraging them to continue on the way. They have discovered the treasure in the field, the kingdom of God, and with joy (*prae gaudio*) they have already sold all they had to buy that field (cf. *Mt*. 13, 44). Benedict encourages those who might have done some backsliding to offer something extra with a joy like the joy they had at the beginning of their religious life. Indeed, at times, they had signs that the kingdom was among them, and they have come to know that hope which will not disappoint because the love of God has been poured out in their hearts through the Holy Spirit who has been given to them" (*JL*, p. 286).

Contrary to society's understanding of joy as a spontaneous emotion, the *Rule* and Scripture tell us that joy can be chosen, can be nurtured, and can be commanded and taught. Fr. Kurt concludes, "A certain type of joy, therefore, can be taught. Christ teaches it in the beatitudes, and the apostles also teach it in other parts of scripture. To tell someone to rejoice in difficult circumstances is to tell him to recognize what is important and how he possesses it already, even if only in hope. The beatitudes are a promise for the future and call one to a firm hope. This joy sometimes becomes more 'affective' when it emerges as a characteristic experience of the fruit of the Holy Spirit and is a result of participation in his life. It is an interior experience and an anticipation of the kingdom of God. It is a reminder that in the midst of the struggle there still remains 'possibility' as 'undetermined future,' or, rather, as a future determined by one's cooperation with the grace and sovereign will of God. This joy is a fundamental element of Benedictine spirituality" (*JL*, p. 286).

It is evident that there are a number of other allusions to joy in other chapters of the *Rule*, sometimes in places that seem least likely. I recently discovered one such instance in Chapter 22, entitled "The Sleeping Arrangements of the Monks." St. Benedict calls the monks to be very ready to rise for Vigils by prescribing that "they sleep clothed, and girded with belts or cords. ... Thus the monks will always be ready to arise without delay when the signal is given; each will hasten to arrive at the Work of God before the others, yet with all dignity and decorum. ...On arising for the Work of God, they will quietly encourage each other, for the sleepy like to make excuses" (RB 22: 5, 6, 8). The word "hasten" implies that the monks are hurrying to participate in something wonderful and appealing, something that should be joyful since the Divine Office is prayed in communion with the saints and angels in heaven and symbolizes our devotion to Christ and our love for Christ and His Church. On the other hand, early rising may not be easy for all the monks; so some must give others encouragement to remind them of their sacred duty and privilege. So, too, today we must remind one another that it is a truly joyful thing and a privilege to pray the Liturgy of the Hours and that we are anticipating the heavenly joy of praising God when we shall be more immediately in the company of saints. (The same could be said about rising early to attend a weekday or a Sunday Mass.) Let us, then, also hasten to the Work of God; let us also encourage one another to overcome spiritual and physical drowsiness so that we might hasten together with joy to this most delightful of earthly endeavors. Was it not the Blessed Mother who hastened with joy "to the hill country" to serve her cousin Elizabeth, to share the Good News of Christ's birth with her, to elicit from her a "loud cry" of joy, and even to inspire John the Baptist in the womb to leap for joy? (cf. Lk 2: 39-45). Then, summarizing this whole experience as well as the Incarnation of her Son and the story of redemption in Christ, Mary goes on to utter her profound song of joyful praise in the Magnificat. All this happens amid the hardships of Mary's long arduous journey, the challenge of Elizabeth's pregnancy in old age, and the tasks of Mary's assistance to Elizabeth over a period of six months. We are indeed privileged to share in her joy if every evening we are able to pray Vespers and include her proclamation: "My soul proclaims the greatness of the Lord; my spirit rejoices in God, my Savior" (Lk 2: 46-47).

In the conclusion of his dissertation, Fr. Kurt mentions the implications of St. Benedict's references to joy for Benedictine life and spirituality—for monks and, in an extended sense, for all of us. Fr. Kurt writes, "First of all, Benedict's summons to joy in Lent asks that one recognize that the monastic life [or any Christian life] is a dynamic *process* of maturity in the Spirit rather than a *state* of perfection. This life is built upon the salvation that God has wrought in Christ's paschal mystery and presumes a generous response to grace" (*JL*, p. 291). "Secondly, to arrive at this maturity, one must give oneself over to the practices or the observances which Benedict recommends to his monks during Lent. They lead one to joy and are not obstacles to it" (*JL*, p. 291). "Thirdly, joy in Lent is tied to a certain spiritual freedom, a tranquility, a peace and calm, and a generosity which are accessible only to those who are willing to submit to a radical transformation of their wills and desires. This they do through unhesitating obedience. ..." (*JL*, p. 191). "Finally, joy in Lent implies an unconditional preference for and attachment to Christ. Joy, love, peace and the other characteristics of the fruit of the Spirit are signs of the life of Christ in the Christian, and in this case, in the monk. To rejoice in Lent really means to struggle constantly against the flesh, to be removed from personal autonomy, and to be attached totally to Christ" (*JL*, pp. 191-192).

Indeed, joy comes to us as a marvelous by-product of our love relationship with Christ. It is the observances of monastic life and the various other practices of Christian discipleship that can help us to cope fruitfully with difficult and painful circumstances and that can open us to the deep, pervasive, lasting joy that is available in every situation. Let us, then, learn to observe these disciplines to which the Lord invites us and to delight in them! The Lord offers them to us for the sake of our joy, which He wishes us to experience during our journeys of faith on earth and to partake of fully in eternity.

CHAPTER 4

The Prevalence of Joy in Various Passages of the Bible

The fifth chapter of Fr. Kurt's dissertation is entitled "Joy in the Bible in Relation to Themes in *RB* 49." Since St. Benedict quoted Scripture so many times, it makes sense to see how his pervasive sense of joy, despite the use of the word *gaudium* only two times, is connected to references to joy throughout the Bible.

There is much rejoicing in the Old Testament; in some passages we even find God rejoicing in us when we are His faithful people! The joy in the New Testament is even deeper since it is based on Christ's Resurrection from the dead and our call to share in the Resurrection. Besides the many references to joy in the writings of St. Paul (see Chapter 5), we find exhortations to rejoice in the angels' message at the Incarnation; in Our Lord's desire to share His joy completely with us, as expressed in the Gospel of St. John; in St. Peter's and St. James' reminders to rejoice in suffering; in the apostles' seemingly irrepressible joy in every situation, even amid the worst of persecutions, in the Acts of the Apostles; and in the general ambiance of the Book of Revelation, which proclaims the ultimate victory of the Lamb on the throne and His faithful ones over evil forces.

Fr. Kurt states that the type of joy that monks are urged to embrace in *RB* 49 is very much in harmony with Biblical exhortations to rejoice. He writes, "Two themes in particular...cannot, therefore, be ignored" (*JL*, pp 2-3). The first theme might be called "discipline." During Lent, which is to be a model for the whole of monastic life, St. Benedict urges his monks to try especially hard to live in purity of heart and "to wash away in this holy season the negligences of other times" (*RB* 49:2-3). A second theme with which we would not automatically associate "joy" is that of "suffering" or "sacrifice." The observances of Lent involve adding "to the usual measure of our service something by way of private prayer and abstinence from food or drink" (*RB* 49:5) and some self-denial regarding "sleep, needless talking and idle jesting" (*RB* 49:7). One might note that the communal observance of Lent already demands a significant sacrifice since in *RB* 41:7, for the Lenten season, St. Benedict moves the single meal of the day from mid-afternoon to the evening. Furthermore, the lengthening daylight during the springtime would cause an even longer wait between one's waking and one's eating the one and only meal allowed for the day.

In the Vulgate version of the Bible, which was known to St. Benedict, there are numerous passages in which occurrences of discipline and suffering are accompanied by joy. In his analyses of passages in the Bible, Father Kurt discovered 150 occurrences of the noun *gaudium* (joy) and 122 occurrences of the verb *gaudere* (rejoice). Of these incidences, twenty-one are related to the themes of *RB* 49. We might categorize these combinations as follows: joy and discipline, joy and sacrifice *per se*, joy and trials in general, and joy in suffering persecution.

Joy occurs with the notion of discipline in three passages. When

St. Paul is reminding the Romans that the Kingdom of God is a matter of "justice, peace, and joy in the Holy Spirit" (Rom 14:17), he is encouraging them to discipline themselves and urging them not to let their practices of eating and drinking cause scandal to the brothers who are weak in faith. Likewise in Galatians, St. Paul proclaims that true freedom is related to the cross; only those who "have crucified their flesh with its passions and desires" belong to Christ and possess the fruits of the Spirit, including joy (Gal 5:22-26). Finally, in Hebrews discipline is said to be a cause for joy, even though at first it seems to be a cause for grief (Heb 12:11). All these passages remind us that genuine joy, far from being a merely spontaneous feeling, arises from the hard work of self-denial for the sake of Christ and for love of others.

Joy also occurs with the notion of sacrifice in a number of passages. During the Last Supper, while Jesus is preparing to lay down His life for His disciples, He proclaims that He is revealing difficult truths to them so that His joy may be in them and that their joy may be complete (Jn 15:11). When Our Lord prays to the Father in Jn 17, He again asks that His disciples might share His joy completely (Jn 17:13). St. Paul tells the Corinthians that, despite great trials, the churches in Macedonia have nonetheless sacrificed themselves to contribute to the collection for the Church in Jerusalem; their abundant generosity came from overflowing joy and deep poverty (2 Cor 8:2). In Colossians St. Paul rejoices in being able to suffer in the flesh for the sake of Christ's Body, the Church (Col. 1:24). In Hebrews Christ is shown to have sacrificed Himself on the cross for the sake of the joy which lay before Him (Heb 12:2). All these passages indicate that only through sacrificial love can genuine joy be tasted.

Joy is linked with the experience of various trials in a number of passages of the Bible. Amid famine and seeming abandonment by God, the prophet Habakkuk promises to rejoice in the Lord and to exult in the God of his salvation (Hab 3:18). In his Letter to the Romans, St. Paul links together the virtues of "rejoicing in hope, being patient under trial, and persevering in prayer" (Rom 12:12). In Second Corinthians he speaks of ministers of the Gospel as rejoicing always even as they are seen as sad (2 Cor 6:10), with the sadness presumably stemming from the trials of Christian ministry. Later he tells of his own joy despite difficulties with the Corinthians' disordered behavior (2 Cor 7:4), and then he professes how he rejoices when he is weak because he finds his strength in Christ (2 Cor 13:9). In Colossians St. Paul prays that the community may endure joyfully whatever trials may come their way (Col 1:11). The Letter of James opens with an instruction that the brothers should consider it pure joy when they are subjected to various trials, for it is then that their faith is tested and their endurance grows (Jas 1:2-4). Yes, trials endured for the love of Christ and arising from efforts to proclaim Him can be occasions of joy.

Finally, Christian joy is also associated even with persecution. Although when he experienced persecution Jeremiah even lamented that he had been born, yet the Lord's words became the joy of his heart when he devoured them (Jer 15:16). In the final beatitude, in the versions of both St. Matthew and St. Luke, Jesus tells the disciples to rejoice when they are persecuted on account of Him (Mt 5:12, Lk 6:23). The apostles, in fact, do just that in Acts when they leave the Sanhedrin rejoicing for having been judged worthy of ill treatment for the sake of Jesus' name (Acts 5:41). Likewise, it was amid persecution that the Thessalonians received the word of God in the joy of the Holy Spirit (1 Thes 1:6). (This probably is the very text to which St. Benedict is alluding in *RB* 49:6.) The community addressed in Hebrews responded with joy to the confiscation of their possessions (Heb 10:34), and those addressed by First Peter are urged to rejoice to the measure in which they share Christ's sufferings (1 Pt 4:13). Certainly, we would not wish ourselves or anyone else persecution, but it is consoling to know the truth that those persecuted for their Christian faith will experience the joy of closer fellowship with Christ.

All these references remind us that only in God, and in Christ in particular, do our hearts find deep and abiding joy. To the amazement of the secularized world, this abundant joy can be discovered in situations of discipline, sacrifice, persecution, and all sorts of other trials.

CHAPTER 5

Saint Paul's Experience of Gospel Joy and Its Connection with the Holy Spirit

F r. Kurt entitled Chapter IV of his dissertation "Joy and the Holy Spirit in the Writings of St. Paul" (pp. 131-149). It makes much sense to look at St. Paul's writings since his reference to joy in 1 Thes 1:6 is the basis for St. Benedict's use of "the joy of the Holy Spirit" in *RB* 49:6. In other letters, too, especially in Philippians, St. Paul expresses his own joy stemming from his conversion and from various experiences in his ministry of evangelization, and he exhorts his various communities to strive to rejoice in a way similar to his own rejoicing. Therefore, we can certainly learn much about joy from St. Paul. In his dissertation Fr. Kurt demonstrates that the theme of joy and the activity of the Holy Spirit are "interwoven in the whole fabric of Pauline theology and that fabric becomes all the more fascinating as one approaches it and finds in its warp and woof patterns too of suffering, hope, and asceticism" (*JL*, p. 141).

For St. Paul to be a Christian is to live in Christ through the Spirit of Christ; it is to "live according to the spirit" (Rom 8:4), the spirit being that dimension of a person which opens himself to the Holy Spirit and to God's very life. Thus the Holy Spirit is the ruling and ordering power of Christians. To be guided by the Spirit and thus to live "in the spirit" is the opposite of being "in the flesh," which is to remain under the dominion of autonomous, selfish forces. Those who live according to the spirit have surrendered their lives to Christ so that the Holy Spirit frees them from the slavery of egoism. This domination of one's life by the Spirit is manifested by love, which is a share in the outpouring of Christ's own love. Living in the spirit is not an automatic state of life, nor is it a once-for-all achievement. Rather, it involves a continual struggle against the flesh and an ever-renewed decision to engage in this struggle, with the grace of God sustaining one's hope and one's efforts. The new mode of being which results from living "in the spirit" results in an experience of deep joy. St. Paul realizes this truth from his own experiences of joy while he is being renewed in Christ over and over. He, therefore, exhorts Christians again and again to rejoice in the Lord (Phil 3:1, 4:4). He urges them to "rejoice always" and to "give thanks in all circumstances" (1 Thes 5:16, 18), even amid great trials. These last two commands are linked with the instruction to "pray without ceasing" (1 Thes 5:17), which is a matter of remaining in Christ and the Holy Spirit perseveringly. This profound Christian joy is found in the context of suffering, of hope, and of asceticism, according to Fr. Kust.

Contrary to normal human intuition, St. Paul's joy seems to be greatest amid trials (cf. *JL*, p. 144). In 2 Cor 7:10 he reports that in all his afflictions he is filled with consolation so that his joy knows no bounds. He rejoices, in particular, in the sufferings which he undergoes for others, as he tells the Colossians (Col 1:24). The "for you" seems to echo the "for you" of the Last Supper narrative in 1 Cor 11:24, so that St. Paul's deep joy comes from a participation in Christ's own sacrifice of self-giving love. This paradoxical joy can abound because the tribulations which surround it form part of the Church's progress in ushering in Christ's rule over the world. Thus St. Paul can be always be rejoicing despite the "sadness" of his ministry (2 Cor 6:10); his trials in ministering to the Corinthians do not put a damper on his great joy (2 Cor 7:7); the churches of Macedonia, despite trials and poverty, overflow with joy and generosity (2 Cor 8:2); and the Thessalonians receive God's words with joy amid trials (1 Thes 1:6). St. Paul's joy was surely infectious!

The Christian joy which St. Paul proclaims is possible because of hope. Thus joy has an "eschatological significance"; that is, it is connected with Christ's ultimate victory, the victory of love over evil, which at the present time can be seen only vaguely, and only in painful struggle at that. However, this hope of God's ultimate victory is reason enough to rejoice. In Rom 12:12 St. Paul calls upon the Romans to rejoice in hope and be patient under trial. It is God, the source of hope, who can "fill them with all joy, and peace in believing" (Rom 15:13). Since afflictions unite us to Christ and help to make God's glory known, Christians can even boast of afflictions (Rom 5:3), which can serve to strengthen them in patience, in tested virtue, and in hope. These very afflictions thus contribute to advancing the Kingdom of God in one's being and in the world. Although this joy "is an austere one since it refers to the invisible and is lived in patience" (JL, p. 6), it is nevertheless authentic and bears the test of time as Christians find it in abundance even amid the painful contradictions of life. Throughout his epistles St. Paul provides a view of Christian life that abounds in joy. This joy is an "eschatological gift" since it results from the saving plan of God revealed in Christ and carried forward by the Holy Spirit. The new era ushered in by Christ gives Christians a sure hope in the ultimate victory of God's love, and so their joy in the Spirit "has the power to overcome all trials and distress" (*JL*, p. 6). It is no mere human emotion but an ever available gift which is an integral dimension of Christ's saving work.

Although Christian joy is not opposed to legitimate earthly joys, it nonetheless requires the subordination of such joys to the main focus of Christian life: preferring Christ above all else and pleasing God in all things. Therefore, nurturing Christian joy demands the practice of an asceticism which helps one to let go of those earthly joys which interfere with living in Christ in any given situation. Since the present world is passing away, St. Paul urges those who rejoice to live as if they were not rejoicing. That is, since the Second Coming is near, Christians should keep themselves as free as possible from rejoicing in passing things so that they can devote themselves completely to lasting values (1 Cor 7:29-35). St. Paul also urges married Christians to avoid entanglement in the typical worldly cares that accompany marriage and calls upon all Christians to keep a necessary inward detachment from things of this world. Pleasing the Lord must be at the center of Christian life; so earthly enjoyments must be put in their proper place lest Christians lose themselves in such passing things and thus imperil their complete devotion to the Lord Jesus.

In sum, St. Paul often recommends to his communities a deep interior joy, which becomes manifest particularly in situations of suffering. Love, joy, and peace are fruits of the Spirit which are experienced by those whose lives are shaped by the word of God and which witness against the fragmented life of the flesh. The life of Christ abiding in the Christian, or "life in the spirit," involves a continual struggle against the flesh in order for one to progress toward total commitment to Christ. This struggle entails a certain joyful asceticism of subordinating earthly attachments to the values of the Kingdom. Because of the love of God poured into their hearts by the Holy Spirit, Christians can remain joyful in this struggle since they put all their hope ultimately in the Kingdom of God, which they seek to advance through their asceticism. Christians rejoice as they look forward to Christ's subjection of all things to Himself (Phil 3:21).

This contrast between the fleeting happiness that comes from living in the flesh and the genuine joy of living in the Spirit is evident in our present-day situation. In his book *The Sacred Conversation: The Art of Catholic Preaching and the New Evangelization*, Fr. Joseph Mele reminds priests and deacons that in their preaching they need to draw people from a very secularized culture to the search for holiness and the joy that comes with it. He writes, "Calling people to holiness is a homiletic essential. ... The call to holiness, at its most basic, is a call to Christ. It is a call to a relationship with him, to live in love with him. And to live in love with Christ is to strive to do God's will in all things, with humility, patience, trust, and deep love. None of those things are accomplished overnight. The slow unfolding of grace in one's life is usually a painful and difficult journey. The closer we grow to Christ, the more painfully aware we become of the depths of our own sin. We are wounded to our core, and because of that we must make a constant and decided effort to continue along the path to holiness" (*SC*, p. 74). This seeking of holiness in ongoing conversion is very countercultural, but it is essential if we are to find the true joy that God intends for us. Fr. Mele continues, "[N]o one can progress in the spiritual life without first discovering [his or her] own insufficiency and poverty. In order to grow closer to God, we all must come to learn that holiness is possible only because of his love, his grace. We have to recognize the depths of our own sin and grasp our inability to practice true discipleship apart from divine assistance. Learning that is never easy or pleasant, but there's no getting around it" (*SC*, p. 75). The call to ongoing conversion in Christ is very different from the way of our secular world. Fr. Mele comments, "All of us now live in a fragmented world.

Shards of disparate truth compete with shards of badly thought out philosophies. Traditions, habits, lifestyles, belief systems—all have been deconstructed by post-modernism. That fragmentation and isolation of truth is the source of much of contemporary culture's angst. That angst, which oftentimes borders on despair, can only be overcome through a restored vision of a unified reality. That's true for the culture and that's true for every man and woman in the pew on Sunday morning. People find joy and peace when they find God, when they see the world as it is, and when they see themselves as they are. They find happiness [joy] when they realize that there is no need for despair, that there is always hope" (SC, p. 75). That virtue of hope and the true joy that goes with it resemble the hope that St. Benedict describes in the seventy-fourth instrument of good works. After a monk—or any Christian—has struggled valiantly (and probably failed often) to live by the first seventy-three "tools" in Chapter 4 of the Rule, St. Benedict offers the beautiful admonition, "And, finally, never lose hope in God's mercy" (RB 4:74). Remembering the constant availability of God's mercy amid our brokenness and failures is a powerful source of Christian joy! In cooperation with St. Paul and St. Benedict, we can by our witness invite the people of our day to partake of this joy.

CHAPTER 6

Joy Expressed in Liturgical Prayers: Both Joy and Sorrow in Lent and Easter

The joy of coming to know Christ more deeply and of living in His presence appears in the prayers and readings of both Lent and Easter. As the *Rule* of St. Benedict tells us, there is anticipatory joy in Lenten preparations for Easter, and there is even the experience of joy in the practice of self-sacrifice out of love for Christ and others since we are sharing in the very sacrificial love of Christ Himself. Likewise, the joy rightly associated with Easter is not without the experience of suffering and unfulfillment. This joy anticipates the fullness of joy that is to be experienced in eternity, and the living and proclaiming of the joy of the Gospel often involves substantial suffering and sometimes even persecution. It is the joy that comes from the sacrificial love of Christ that sustains us in prayer and work amid all the trials of Christian life.

Hints of Joy during the Season of Lent

Even on Ash Wednesday, as we begin a time of "holy fasting," a "campaign of Christian service," and an especially intense "battle against spiritual evils" (Opening Prayer for Ash Wednesday), we hear in the Responsorial Psalm the words of Psalm 51: "Give me back the joy of your salvation, and a willing spirit sustain in me" (Ps 51: 14). That psalm and that verse occur also in a number of Masses throughout the Season of Lent. Furthermore, Our Lord Himself exhorts us, "When you fast, do not look gloomy like the hypocrites" (Mt 6:16). It is clear that He wants us to fast with cheerfulness and joyful self-giving.

Preface I for Lent reminds us that Lent is indeed a joyful season, even if the joy experienced is largely anticipatory. The preface's prayer reads: "For by your [the Father's] gracious gift each year your faithful await the sacred paschal feasts with the joy of minds made pure, so that, more eagerly intent on prayer and on the works of charity and participating in the mysteries by which they have been reborn, they may be led to the fullness of grace that you bestow on your sons and daughters." This prayer helps us to enter into the understanding of the true joy of growing closer to Christ in His mysteries, of having our minds purified of less worthy things, of gaining a greater taste for prayer, and of growing in zeal for deeds of love performed in Christ's name. This joy also anticipates the joy of heaven, where we shall experience the "fullness of grace."

Preface II of the Passion, used on Monday, Tuesday, and Wednesday of Holy Week, also anticipates Easter joy in its prayer: "For the days of his [Christ's] saving Passion and glorious Resurrection are approaching, by which the pride of the ancient foe is vanquished and the mystery of our redemption in Christ is celebrated." Yes, there is even joy in our painful struggles against the devil's schemes since, with God's grace, we thus enter into Christ's redeeming love—and His own struggle against Satan—again and again.

Other liturgical prayers throughout the Lenten Season also express the theme of joy. Sometimes this theme appears in the optional Prayer over the People (recited after the Prayer after Communion and the final greeting), and we need to be especially attentive to it when it is used since we may be eager to depart as the Mass approaches its end. This prayer for the Saturday for the First Week of Lent reads: "May the blessing for which they have longed strengthen your faithful, O God, so that, never straying from your will, they may always rejoice in your benefits." On Tuesday of the Second Week of Lent, the prayer reads: "Graciously hear the cries of your faithful, O Lord, and relieve the weariness of their souls, that, having received your forgiveness, they may ever rejoice in your blessing." The theme of joy also appears in the collects, the prayers over the gifts, and the prayers after communion on various days of Lent. The Collect on the Second Sunday of Lent, when Gospels about the Transfiguration of the Lord are proclaimed in all three cycles, reads: "O God, who have commanded us to listen to your beloved Son, be pleased, we pray, to nourish us inwardly by your word, that, with spiritual sight made pure, we may rejoice to behold your glory." Although our beholding of the fullness of God's glory will be possible only in heaven, we can pray to enjoy, even now, occasional glimpses of that glory— yes, even during Lent. On Monday of the Second Week of Lent, we hear the following words of the Prayer after Communion: "May this Communion, O Lord, cleanse us of wrongdoing and make us heirs to the joy of heaven." We are also warned not to become absorbed in earthly happiness; the Prayer over the Offerings on the Thursday of the Third Week of Lent includes the phrase, "Do not let them [Your people] cling to false joys."

Furthermore, many words and phrases in other liturgical prayers during Lent imply situations of joy. Such themes as looking forward to glory and eternal life and salvation in Christ occur frequently. Some examples of joy-filled phrases are: "glorious healing remedies … on earth," "lifted up by your mercy," "solace in this life," "that… we may be gladdened by [the] full effects [of the paschal mysteries]." Of course, on "Laetare Sunday," the Fourth Sunday of Lent (*laetare* is Latin for "rejoice"), we find many reminders of the spiritual joy that we are invited to experience. The Entrance Antiphon begins with the words, "Rejoice, Jerusalem." The Prayer over the Offerings reads: "We place before you with joy these offerings, which bring eternal remedy, O Lord, praying that we may both faithfully revere them and present them to you, as is fitting, for the salvation of all the world." The Communion Antiphon for Year C, when the Gospel of the Prodigal Son is read, begins with the phrase "You must rejoice, my son," which reflects the father's appeal to his older son: "'But now we must celebrate and rejoice, because your brother was dead and has come to life again; he was lost and has been found'" (Lk 15:32). On the Solemnity of Saint Joseph, usually in the midst of Lent, the people are summoned to "rejoice" in the day's solemn Eucharistic celebration after they have been "nourished with food from this altar" (Prayer after Communion).

During Lent a number of readings prescribed for Mass show forth themes of joy. On Monday of the First Week of Lent, we hear the Gospel of the Last Judgment (Mt 25:31-46), in which "the Son of Man comes in his glory" (25:31) and those who practice works of mercy are invited to "inherit the kingdom prepared for you from the foundation of the world" (25:34). The Responsorial Psalm on the next day includes the phrase, "Look to him [the Lord] that you may be radiant with joy" (Ps 34:6). That Thursday we hear in the Gospel about "your heavenly Father," who gives "good things to those who ask him" (Mt 7:11). On the Third Sunday of Lent, Year A, we hear the

Gospel about the Samaritan woman, who after her encounter with Christ, runs joyfully to her townspeople to share her grace-filled experience with them and thus to evangelize (cf. Jn 4: 28-30). On that same Sunday, St. Paul tells us that through Christ "we have gained access by faith to this grace in which we stand, and we boast in hope of the glory of God" (Rom 5:2). On Monday of the Fourth Week of Lent, the prophet Isaiah proclaims that the Lord is "about to create new heavens and a new earth" (Is 65:17), in which "there shall always be rejoicing and happiness" (65:18), since He has created "Jerusalem to be a joy and its people to be a delight" (65:18). Furthermore, the Lord proclaims, "I will rejoice in Jerusalem and exult in my people" (Is 65:19). It is wonderful and genuinely consoling to know that the Lord Himself rejoices when we respond faithfully to Him and open ourselves to His lavish gifts. Throughout Lent we thus hear Scriptures that promise abundant graces to those who repent and come to know Christ and also promise the joyful reward of eternal life to those who remain faithful to Him.

Expressions of Joy amid Suffering during the Easter Season

One thinks of the Easter Season as a time of joy, and indeed it is. We rejoice in Christ's Resurrection and our share in it through the promise of eternal life. We rejoice in the Holy Spirit's guidance to a deeper, richer life in Christ. We rejoice in the forgiveness of sins given to us through the Holy Spirit and the Sacrament of Reconciliation, established by Our Lord for us on the evening of Easter Sunday. This joy, however, is only a foreshadowing of the fullness of joy that awaits us in heaven. Furthermore, this joy, in order to be genuine, needs to be tested by all sorts of trials, as shown by the various persecutions and other severe trials experienced by believers in the early Church.

In the prayers of the Church during Easter, we hear phrases expressing the need for discipline and perseverance through suffering, such as "hold fast ... to the Sacraments," "that ... they may never lose what they have received," and "drawn [away] from earthly desires." On the Wednesday of the Octave of Easter we hear the Prayer after Communion: "We pray, O Lord, that the reverent reception of the Sacrament of your Son may cleanse us from our old ways and transform us into a new creation." Yes, even though it may be Easter, we are still tempted to be stuck in "old ways," and the ongoing tenacity of sinful patterns of the past require us to engage in an ongoing struggle against the "old man."

One option for the second reading for Easter Sunday calls us to "clear out the old yeast," that is "the yeast of malice and wickedness" (1 Cor 5:7, 8). In the accounts of the Resurrection proclaimed during the Octave, the disciples are slow to believe and need to take to heart the risen Lord's reproaches in order to overcome their fears and sorrows and to come to delight in His greetings of peace and joy. However, once they overcome these obstacles and become filled with the Holy Spirit, they can endure all sorts of suffering with a purified and enduring joy. When Saints Peter and John are brought before the Jewish leaders, who are angry with them for preaching the Gospel and for healing in the name of Christ, the two apostles refuse to give in to warnings "not to speak or teach at all in the name of Jesus" (Acts 4:18). Instead, they proclaim with joyful courage, "It is impossible for us not to speak about what we have seen and heard" (Acts 4:20). (This passage occurs on the Saturday of the Octave of Easter.) Perhaps most remarkable are two passages from the Acts of the Apostles that show the apostles rejoicing amidst opposition and punishment. St. Peter and the other apostles are often imprisoned and brought before the court. On Thursday of the Second Week of Easter, we hear that the Jewish high priest scolds them for continuing to preach in Jesus' name. The apostles say in reply, "'We must obey God rather than men'" (Acts 5:29). The reading for the next day narrates that the court officials "had them [the apostles] flogged, ordered them to stop speaking in the name of Jesus, and dismissed them." In response, the apostles "left the presence of the Sanhedrin, rejoicing that they had been found worthy to suffer dishonor for the sake of the name [of Jesus]" (Acts 5:40-41). The other remarkable incident, read on the Saturday of the Fourth Week of Easter, involves the apostles Paul and Barnabas as they proclaim the Gospel in Antioch of Pisidia. After the Gentiles of the city received God's word with delight, some Jews of the town stirred up a persecution and expelled the two missionaries from their territory. The response of the rejected apostles displayed amazing courage and joy: "So they shook the dust from their feet in protest against them and went to Iconium. The disciples were filled with joy and the Holy Spirit" (Acts 13:51-52). It seems that these early evangelists were so caught up in the joy of the Gospel and their lively relationship with Christ that no frustration could hinder them from rejoicing.

On Sundays of Easter in Year A, we hear from the First Letter of St. Peter, which speaks much of suffering with and for Christ and of suffering with joy. On the Second Sunday we hear: "In this [the new birth coming to us through the Resurrection] you rejoice, although now for a little while you may have to suffer through various trials, so that the genuineness of your faith … may prove to be for praise, glory, and honor at the revelation of Jesus Christ" (1 Pt 1:7). Furthermore, because of this Easter faith, "you rejoice with an indescribable and glorious joy, as you attain the goal of your faith, the salvation of your souls" (1 Pt 1:9). St. Peter tells us on the Fourth Sunday, "If you are patient when you suffer for doing what is good, this is a grace before God" (1 Pt 2:20). Such patient suffering is very possible and is, in fact, a privilege "because Christ also suffered for you, leaving you an example that you should follow in his footsteps" (2:21). On the Sixth Sunday, we hear St. Peter tell us, "For it is better to suffer for doing good, if that be the will of God, than for doing evil" (3:17). Again, such suffering is borne in imitation of Christ, who "also suffered for sins once ... that he might lead you to God" (3:18). The passage from First Peter for the Seventh Sunday might be considered a beautiful little homily on Christian suffering. It reads, in part: "Beloved: Rejoice to the extent that you share in the sufferings of Christ, so that when his glory is revealed you may also rejoice exultantly. If you are insulted for the name of Christ, blessed are you, for the Spirit of glory and of God rests upon you. ... [W]hover is made to suffer as a Christian should not be ashamed but glorify God because of the name" (4:13-16). Also, on the Feast of St. Mark, which always occurs during the Easter Season, we hear St. Peter remind us of the glory that awaits us after this time of suffering. The Christian must know "that your brothers and sisters throughout the world undergo the same sufferings" (5:9). St. Peter sums up the call to future glory by stating, "The God of all grace who called you to his eternal glory through Christ Jesus will himself restore, confirm, strengthen, and establish you after you have suffered a little" (5:11).

All these lessons from St. Peter are very relevant to us today. Did not he himself learn to live in genuine joy partly as a result of his earlier failures and inadequacy as a disciple? Did not Our Lord's reprimands help him to let go of his false joys connected with distorted views about Christ's mission? Indeed, St. Peter gradually learned to find joy in the surrender of his will to Christ's will and thus to God's gracious plan for the Messiah, for Peter himself, and for the whole Church. (I might recommend the book *Into His Likeness* by Edward Sri [Ignatius Press and Augustine Institute, 2017], which very convincingly describes St. Peter's transformation.) Can we not also learn to let go of false joys from our failures, inadequacies, and fears that limit the intensity of our faith? Can we not accept the grace to embrace the genuine joy that comes from abiding in Christ and from bearing patiently with whatever sufferings are entailed? Armed with true joy and the Holy Spirit who bestows it on us, we can persevere through all sorts of trials without losing this enduring Christian joy. This disposition is that of Easter faith in its fullness, which prepares us for the unsurpassable joy of heaven. Yes, in the risen Christ may our hearts always rejoice!

Easter (and Sabbath) Joy as Incomplete in Our Experiences

It is a Christian teaching that every Sunday is a celebration of Easter in miniature. As indicated in the *Rule* of St. Benedict and in Church documents, Sunday should be a day devoted to public worship, extra personal prayer, rejuvenating leisurely activities, and efforts to strengthen ties in family and community. During the initial phase of the coronavirus pandemic, from mid-March through May of 2020, there were no public Masses in most dioceses, including our diocese, and other religious activities had to be canceled as well. Although I missed the opportunity to minister to people in parishes and to gather with Oblates of St. Benedict at meetings, the deprivation gave me a different opportunity—to experience a fuller "Sabbath" on Sundays. However, I came to realize that with much more free time to pray, to write letters to family and friends, and to do spiritual reading and light reading, I always fell short of my goals for any given Sunday. (As I often do during the work week, it is undoubtedly my fault for planning too much and thus setting myself up for disappointment!) At the same time, there was a memorable lesson gained from this phenomenon. No matter how wonderful an experience of Sabbath leisure we may have on this earth, something is still lacking. This insufficiency reminds us that the fullness of joy is found only when we shall share completely, body and soul, in the life of our risen Lord at the time of the resurrection of our bodies.

Yes, we should have joy during Lent amid our disciplines and in our deeper entry into the Passion of Christ. Yes, we should have joy during Easter in our renewed appreciation of communion with the risen Christ. However, the joy in Lent always points to the joy of Easter, and the joy of Easter always points to the joy of eternal life in heaven. Finding our joy in abiding in Christ, in heeding His words, and in doing His will, we shall come to realize how imperfect is our communion with Him on earth and how we need to strive ever more valiantly for the "prize" held in store for us in heaven. Rather than be discouraged by the limitations on our joy on earth, weighed down as our life is with earthly cares, we need all the more to welcome God's gift of encouragement to "progress in this way of life and in faith" and thus to "run on the path of God's commandments, our hearts overflowing with the inexpressible delight of love" (*RB* Prol.: 49). St. Benedict assures us at the very end of the *Rule* that if we set out for the loftier summits set before us, then under God's grace and protection we shall reach them! (cf. *RB* 73:9).

CHAPTER 7

Christian Joy as Expressed in Documents of Recent Popes

The seeking of true Christian joy is very much a part of the "new evangelization" promoted by recent popes. In his book *The Noonday Devil: Acedia, the Unnamed Evil of Our Times*, Abbot Jean-Charles Nault, O.S.B., in the chapter "The New Evangelization against Acedia," quotes from Pope Benedict XVI's homily for the opening of the Year of Faith in 2012: "'Recent decades have seen the advance of a spiritual 'desertification.' In the Council's time it was already possible from a few tragic pages of history to know what a life or a world without God looked like, but now we see it every day around us. This void has spread. But it is in starting from the experience of this desert, from this void, that we can again discover the joy of believing, its vital importance for us men and women. In the desert we rediscover the value of what is essential for living; thus in today's world there are innumerable signs, often expressed implicitly or negatively, of the thirst for God, for the ultimate meaning of life. ... Living faith opens the heart to the grace of God which frees us from pessimism ...'" (*ND*, p. 199). Abbot Jean-Charles goes on to say, "These situations—spiritual desert, lack of joy and hope, general discouragement—are sometimes so tragic that they attack the very fiber of our Christian communities, subtly spreading the sickness of acedia, as Pope Paul VI already acknowledged" (*ND*, p. 199). The author then quotes Pope St. Paul VI from his apostolic exhortation *Evangelii nuntiandi* from December 8, 1975 (no. 80): "such obstacles [to evangelization] are also present today, and we shall limit ourselves to mentioning the lack of fervor. It is all the more serious because it comes from within. It is manifested in fatigue, disenchantment, compromise, lack of interest and above all lack of joy and hope" (*ND*, p. 200). The author continues: "Therefore we urgently need to announce the Good News of salvation joyfully. ... However, in this context, the new evangelization is proposed, not as a duty, an additional burden to carry, but as a remedy that can restore joy and life to realities that are imprisoned by our fears" (*ND*, pp. 200-201). Again Abbot Jean-Charles quotes Pope St. Paul VI's exhortation: "... May it [the task of evangelizing] be the great joy of our consecrated lives. And may the world of our time, which searching, sometimes with anguish, sometimes with hope, be enabled to receive the Good News not from evangelizers who are dejected, discouraged, impatient or anxious, but from ministers of the Gospel whose lives glow with fervor, who have first received the joy of Christ" (*ND*, p. 201). In summarizing the theme of his book, the author then states, "We have had many occasions to say it in these pages: the chief remedy for acedia is found in the joy of the gift. A gift that precedes us, which is the gift of God himself who has come to be united with his creature, to share his weakness and poverty, so as to lead him to the ultimate goal of his existence: sharing in the very life of God" (*ND*, p. 201).

So important to Pope St. Paul VI was the need for joy in our Church and our world that he wrote an entire document on this topic: *On Christian Joy* (apostolic exhortation, *Gaudete in Domino* in Latin, May 9, 1975). In his first section, "The need for joy in all people's hearts," Pope Paul stated that "there are several degrees of … 'happiness'" and that "its most noble expression is joy, or 'happiness' in the strict sense, when man, on the level of his higher faculties, finds his peace and satisfaction in the possession of a known and loved good" (p. 2, with reference to St. Thomas Aquinas, *Summa Theologica*, I-II, q. 31, a. 3). This genuine spiritual joy is experienced most fully when one's spirit "enters into possession of God, known and loved as the supreme and immutable good" (p. 2, with reference to *Summa Theologica*, II-III, q. 28, na. 1,4). It is especially difficult to attain this joy in our present age because although "technological society has succeeded in multiplying the opportunities for pleasure, … it has great difficulty in generating joy. For joy comes another source… It is spiritual" (p. 2). Nevertheless, Pope Paul discerned the need, all the more, not to be hindered "from speaking about joy and hoping for joy. It is indeed in the midst of their distress that our fellow men need to know joy, to hear its song" (p. 3). Man enters into this joy, the Holy Father said, "by becoming more present to God [and] by turning away from sin" (pp. 3-4).

In his exhortation Pope Paul then went on to reflect on joy in the Old Testament and the New Testament, with emphasis on "the secret of the unfathomable joy which dwells in Jesus and which is special to Him" (p. 6). It is a joy based on Christ's relationship with the Father. Furthermore, "the disciples and all those who believe in Christ are called to share in this joy" (p. 6). "The message of Jesus promises above all joy—this demanding joy," which begins with the beatitudes and springs "from the simultaneous celebration of the death and resurrection of the Lord" (p. 7). This joy is "properly spiritual," and is experienced as "a fruit of the Holy Spirit" (p. 7). Saints experienced such joy even amid great suffering. As one example, Pope Paul cited St. Maximilian Kolbe, who "offered himself voluntarily to death in order to save an unknown brother, and the witnesses reported that his interior peace, serenity and joy somehow transformed the place of suffering, which was usually like an image of hell, into the antechamber of eternal life, both for his unfortunate companions and for himself" (p. 10). In a section entitled "A joy for all the people," the Holy Father showed how responding to the call to orient oneself to the supernatural is possible for all human beings and thus also makes possible the summons to experience Christian joy. Even those "who feel your heart divided when God's call reaches you" (p. 11) are not to be discouraged from seeking this joy; St. Paul VI stated that "we feel that our joy, like yours, will only be complete if we look together, with full confidence, to [Christ]" (p. 11), our Lord who "endured the cross, disregarding the shamefulness of it" (p. 11, quoting from Heb 12:2-3). Children "are apt subjects for Gospel Joy" insofar as they develop their "capacity for welcoming, for wonderment, for confidence and for spontaneous giving" (p. 11). People who have heavy, burdensome responsibilities must know that "the Holy Spirit wants to help [them to] rediscover these [daily] joys, to purify them, to share them" (p. 11). Even people who suffer greatly, especially "those who have reached the evening of their lives," need to know that "God's joy is knocking at the door of their physical and moral sufferings" and inviting them to embrace "His paradoxical work of transfiguration" (p. 11). People who are not Christian, "[by] bringing their lives into harmony with the innermost appeal of their conscience, which is the echo of God's voice, ... are on the road to joy" (pp. 11-12). Called in a special way to help others "take the paths of Gospel joy" are "pastors, the theologians, the spiritual directors, the priests and those who collaborate with them in the animation of Christian communities" (p. 12). Joy is available in a special way to sinners who learn of God's mercy. In particular, "frequent confession remains a privileged source of holiness, peace and joy" (p. 12).

Among all these categories of people and in all these situations, circumstances which might not naturally seem to be channels of joy become opportunities for joy when Christ is welcomed to enter, for He indeed is our joy. After calling young people to share in genuine joy and referring to the joy of pilgrimage in the holy year 1975, Pope Paul reflected on the supreme joy of participation in the Holy Eucharist. "[All] the leaders and animators of the Christian communities" need not to "be afraid to insist time and time again on the need for baptized Christians to be faithful to the Sunday celebration, in joy, of the Eucharist" (p. 17). The Eucharist "is the culmination here below of the alliance of love between God and His people: the sign and source of Christian joy, the preparation for the eternal feast" (p. 17).

Pope St. John Paul II, in his many writings and speeches in the course of over twenty-six years as Supreme Pontiff, addressed the concept of Christian joy on numerous occasions and in numerous documents. In his encyclical *Rich in Mercy*, the Holy Father referred to the fidelity and joy expressed by the father of the prodigal son. He wrote: "The father of the Prodigal Son is faithful to his fatherhood, faithful to the love that he had always lavished on his son. This fidelity is expressed in the parable not only by his immediate readiness to welcome him home when he returns after having squandered his inheritance; it is expressed even more fully by that joy, that merry-making for the squanderer after his return, merry-making which is so generous that it provokes the opposition and hatred of the elder brother ..." (*RM*, p. 20). Pope John Paul continued, "The father first and foremost expresses to him his joy that he has been 'found again' and that he has 'returned to life.' This joy indicates a good that has remained intact: even if he is a prodigal, a son does not cease to be truly his father's son; it also indicates a good that has been found again, which in the case of the Prodigal Son was his return to the truth about himself" (*RM*, p. 21). Near the end of the document, the Holy Father asserted, "In analyzing the parable of the Prodigal Son, we have already called attention to the fact that he who forgives and he who is forgiven encounter one another at an essential point, namely the dignity or essential value of the person, a point which cannot be lost and the affirmation of which, or its rediscovery, is a source of the greatest joy" (*RM*, p. 49). These reflections remind us of the joy of confessing our sins, the joy of Lent, the joy of doing acts of penance that help us to repent of sin, and the joy of growing in the knowledge of the Father's all-faithful love. This joy involves the painful hard work of turning away from sin, but it far exceeds any pleasure that we might derive from immersion in sinful behavior. In fact, this joy is shared by God Himself and by His angels and saints, as Our Lord says in the two parables preceding the Parable of the Prodigal Son: "I tell you, ... there will be more joy in heaven over one sinner who repents than over ninety-nine righteous people who have no need of repentance" (Lk 15:7). This rejoicing is so significant that Our Lord reiterates the point: "... I tell you, there will be rejoicing among the angels of God over one sinner who repents" (Lk 15:10).

In his apostolic letter preparing for the celebration of the beginning of the Third Millennium, *Tertio Millennio Adveniente*," Pope St. John Paul pointed to the inner joy and the outer joy that he hoped would characterize the "Jubilee of the Year 2000": "The term 'Jubilee' speaks of joy—not just an inner joy but a jubilation which is manifested outwardly, for the coming of God is also an outward, visible, audible and tangible event, as Saint John makes clear (cf. 1 Jn 1:1). It is thus appropriate that every sign of joy at this coming should have its own outward expression. This will demonstrate that the Church rejoices in salvation. She invites everyone to rejoice, and tries to create conditions to ensure that the power of salvation may be shared by all. Hence the Year 2000 will be celebrated as the Great Jubilee" (*TMA*, pp. 22-23). It is notable that, as the year 2000 approached, much of the secular world, and even many Christians, expressed fear over the malfunctioning of computers and other possible disasters that were predicted to occur at the turn of the millennium. In contrast, the Holy Father, representing the Church and recommending an authentic disposition for Christians, spoke of inward and outward joy. Even while he acknowledged the onerous problems facing the Church and the world, he emphasized that Christian hope demands that we address even the most serious difficulties with the genuine joy that comes from God Himself.

In a culture that often sees children as a burden and that in millions of instances seeks to abort unborn children who are not wanted, Pope St. John Paul II proclaimed the deep joy that should accompany the birth of every human being. In the introduction to his encyclical *The Gospel of Life*, the Holy Father compared the birth of every child with the birth of Our Savior Himself: "At the dawn of salvation, it is the Birth of a Child which is proclaimed as joyful news: 'I bring you good news of a great joy which will come to all the people; for to you is born this day in the city of David a Saviour, who is Christ the Lord' (Lk 2:10-11). The source of this 'great joy' is the Birth of the Saviour; but Christmas also reveals the full meaning of every human birth, and the joy which accompanies the Birth of the Messiah is thus seen to be the foundation and fulfillment of joy at every child born into the world (cf. Jn 16:21)" (*EV*, p. 3). Of course, birth always involves pain, but that pain is far surpassed by the natural—and also spiritual—joy of having a new child of God coming into the world as a sign of His love and as a sign of the new birth that Christ desires for all of us as we undertake our daily journeys of ongoing conversion.

Near the end of the document, Pope John Paul quoted Pope Paul VI in referring to the necessity of the defense and promotion of life if there is to be true peace; the quote, taken from Pope Paul's "Message for the 1977 World Day of Peace," includes the statement, "[W] here human rights are truly professed and publicly recognized and defended, peace becomes the joyful and operative climate of life in society'" (*EV,* p. 181). Finally, St. John Paul concluded his document with a prayer to the Blessed Virgin Mary, including the petition, "Grant that all who believe in your Son may *proclaim the Gospel of life* with honesty and love to the people of our time. Obtain for them the grace to *accept the Gospel* as a gift ever new, the joy *of celebrating* it with gratitude throughout their lives ..." (*EV,* p. 188).

In one of his last documents, the encyclical letter *Ecclesia de Eucharistia* (*On the Eucharist and Its Relationship to the Church,* April 17, 2003), Pope St. John Paul expressed his joy in the Eucharist and his desire that it be celebrated with dignity and effectiveness. In the very beginning of the letter, he asserted that in the Holy Eucharist the Church "joyfully experiences the constant fulfillment of the promise: 'Lo, I am with you always, to the close of the age' (Mt 28:20), but in the Holy Eucharist, through the changing of bread and wine into the body and blood of the Lord, she rejoices in this presence with unique intensity" (*EE,* p. 1; #1). He also expressed the joy of Eucharistic adoration and of Eucharistic processions. In paragraph 10 of the document, Pope John Paul stated, "The devout participation of the faithful in the Eucharistic procession on the Solemnity of the Body and Blood of Christ is a grace from the Lord which yearly brings joy to those who take part in it" (*EE,* p. 9, #10). The Holy Father's joy was mixed with the pain of noticing the neglect of Eucharistic adoration in some places and the abuses that have occurred in some celebrations of the Eucharist (*EE,* #10, p. 9). He concluded the letter on a note of joyful reflection on the future glory of which the Eucharist is a pledge, as even now "Christ walks beside us as our strength and our food for the journey" (*EE,* p. 68, #62). Pope John Paul then ended with the words of a Eucharistic hymn by

St. Thomas Aquinas, which he introduced by saying, "Let us make our own the words of Saint Thomas Aquinas, an eminent theologian and an impassioned poet of Christ in the Eucharist, and turn in hope to the contemplation of that goal to which our hearts aspire in their thirst for joy and peace" (*EE*, p. 68, #62).

It would probably be impossible to cite all the references to spiritual joy in the writings of Pope Benedict XVI before, during, and after his pontificate. He ended his major work *Introduction to Christianity* on a joyful note after he referred to the false but tempting belief that human history is doomed to repeat itself in a circular fashion. Instead, the future Pope said, "Even the Christian may be assailed by the nightmares, induced by the fear of fruitlessness, out of which the pre-Christian world created these moving images of the anxiety that all human activity is vain. But this nightmare is pierced by the saving, transforming voice of reality: 'Be of good cheer, I have overcome the world' (Jn 16:33). The new world, with the description of which, in the image of the final Jerusalem, the Bible ends, is no Utopia but certainty, which we advance to meet in faith. A salvation of the world does exist—that is the confidence that supports the Christian and that still makes it rewarding even today to be a Christian" (*IC*, p. 359). In his book *Behold the Pierced One*, which consists of meditations on the Passion and death of Our Lord, Cardinal Ratzinger concluded his meditation "'The Lamb Redeemed the Sheep': Reflections on the Symbolism of Easter" with the words: "Easter … invites us not only to listen to Jesus but also, as we do so, to develop our interior sight. This greatest festival of the Church's year encourages us, by looking at him who was slain and is risen, to discover the place where heaven is opened. If we comprehend the message of the Resurrection, we recognize that heaven is not completely sealed off above the earth. Then—gently and yet with immense power—something of the light of God penetrates our life. Then we shall feel the surge of joy for which, otherwise, we wait in vain. Everyone who is penetrated by something of this joy can be, in his own way, a window through which heaven can look upon earth and visit it. In this way, what Revelation foresees can come about: every creature in heaven and on earth and under the earth and in the sea, everything in the world is filled with the joy of the redeemed (cf. Rev. 5:13)" (*BPO*, p. 121).

Pope Benedict, like other popes, was especially assiduous in doing what he could to ensure that the Church's priests, who daily celebrate Christ's Death and Resurrection at Mass, be filled with Gospel joy. In his first meditation in *Behold the Pierced One*, "There Are Always Seeds That Bear Fruit for the Harvest," the Holy Father wrote, "But even for the priest the grain of wheat does not simply point to the cross. For him too it is a sign of God's joy. To be able to be the grain of wheat, the servant of the divine grain of wheat Jesus Christ, can at the same time make man glad in the depths of his heart. In the midst of weakness the triumph of grace is fulfilled, as once again we have heard in the epistle from Paul, who experienced the immense joy of God precisely in his wretchedness. Not without embarrassment does the priest learn how through his weak and petty words people can smile in the last moment of their life; how through what he says people find meaning again in the ocean of meaninglessness, meaning on the basis of which they are able to live; and he learns how through him God does great things, through his very weakness, and is full of joy that God has found someone as mean as him worthy of such mercy. And in learning this he becomes at the same time aware that God's joyful wedding feast, his harvest of a hundredfold, is not just a promise in the future but has already begun among us in this bread that he is empowered to distribute, to transform. ... We want to ask God that he will always let something of the splendour of this joy, if it is necessary, fall on our life; that he may give the radiance of this joy ever more deeply and purely to this priest who today for the first time comes before the altar of God; that he will still continually shine upon him when he does so for the last time, when he comes before the altar of eternity in which God shall be the joy of our eternal life, our never-ending youth. Amen" (*MYJ*, pp. 22-23).

In his post-synodal apostolic exhortation *Verbum Domini (The Word of the Lord),* Pope Benedict urged all Christians to experience renewed encounters with Christ through the word of God in the Bible. Reflecting on the synod that preceded his apostolic exhortation, the Pope declared, "Before all else, I would like to call to mind the beauty and pleasure of the renewed encounter with the Lord Jesus which we experienced during the synodal assembly" (*VD*, p. 2, #2). Quoting from the First Letter of St. John, he continued, "The Apostle speaks to us of *hearing, seeing, touching and looking upon* (cf. 1 Jn 1:1) the word of life, since life itself was made manifest in Christ. Called to communion with God and among ourselves, we must proclaim this gift. From this kerygmatic standpoint, the synodal assembly was a testimony, before the Church and before the world, to the immense beauty of encountering the word of God in the communion of the Church. For this reason I encourage all the faithful to renew their personal and communal encounter with Christ, the word of life made visible, and to become his heralds, so that the gift of divine life—communion—can spread ever more fully throughout the world. Indeed, sharing in the life of God, a Trinity of love, is *complete joy* (cf. 1 Jn 1:4). And it is the Church's gift and unescapable duty to communicate that joy, born of an encounter with the person of Christ, the Word of God in our midst" (*VD*, p. 2, #3).

Those who practice *lectio divina* know that it often seems like a chore, and even listening to the word of God at Mass or communal prayer can often be difficult; yet Pope Benedict reminds us that it is a joy, no matter how trying it may feel, to encounter Christ in the words of the Bible. Toward the end of his exhortation, in the section "The word and joy" (pp. 177-178), Pope Benedict asserted, "The greater our openness to God's word, the more will we be able to recognize that today too the mystery of Pentecost is taking place in God's Church. ...This proclamation has been shared with us—the Apostle John reminds us—so that 'our joy may be complete' (1 Jn 1:4). The synodal assembly enabled us to experience all that Saint John speaks of: the proclamation of the word creates *communion* and brings about *joy*. This is a profound joy which has its origin in the very heart of the Trinitarian life and which is communicated to us in the Son. This joy is an ineffable gift which the world cannot give. Celebrations can be organized, but not joy. According to the Scripture, joy is the fruit of the Holy Spirit (cf. Gal 5:22) who enables us to enter into the word and enables the divine word to enter into us and to bear fruit for eternal life. By proclaiming God's word in the power of the Holy Spirit, we also wish to share the source of true joy, not a superficial and fleeting joy, but the joy born of the awareness that the Lord Jesus alone has words of everlasting life (cf. Jn 6:68)" (*VD*, pp. 177-178, #123). In the final section, Pope Benedict addressed the "close relationship between God's word and joy" (*VD*, p. 178, #124) as it is evident in Mary, the Mother of God, especially in her receiving of God's Word at the Annunciation and then in her sharing of that Word with St. Elizabeth and St. John the Baptist (in the womb) during the Visitation. This joy is obviously not a fleeting, intellectually or emotionally satisfying impulse but the true, enduring joy that accompanies a deepening fellowship with Christ, the very Word of God. Undoubtedly, in her intercession for us, the Blessed Mother wishes us to share in this joy.

Pope Francis has often declared that Christians should radiate joy as a people redeemed by Christ. He has also warned that no one will be attracted to the Christian faith by a Christian who has a sour face or a melancholic disposition. In his apostolic exhortation

The Joy of the Gospel: On the Proclamation of the Gospel in Today's World, the Holy Father repeated over and again that world needs true Christian joy and that every Christian must take part in the "new evangelization" of bringing Christ—and His joy—to others. At the beginning of his document, Pope Francis stated, "Whenever our interior life becomes caught up in its own interests and concerns, there is no longer room for others, no place for the poor. God's voice is no longer heard, the quiet joy of his love is no longer felt, and the desire to do good fades. This is a very real danger for believers too. Many fall prey to it, and end up resentful, angry and listless" (*EG*, #2, p. 7). In contrast, the Holy Father summons all Christians to experience "a renewed personal encounter with Jesus Christ" (#3, p. 7), who alone can bring us true joy. In fact, "[n]o one should think that this invitation is not meant for him or her since 'no one is excluded from the joy brought by the Lord'" (#3, p. 8) (quote from Pope St. Paul VI's apostolic exhortation *Gaudete in Domino)*. Pope Francis went on to refer to God's boundless love and mercy from the Gospel and proclaimed, "No one can strip us of the dignity bestowed upon us by this boundless and unfailing love" (#3, p. 8). A few paragraphs later, the Holy Father stated, "The Gospel, radiant with the glory of Christ's cross, constantly invites us to rejoice" (#5, p. 10). He then cited the Blessed Mother's receiving the message "Rejoice" from the angel Gabriel, St. John the Baptist's leaping for joy at the Visitation, Mary's expression of joy in her Magnificat, St. John's finding joy in his decrease while Christ increases (Jn 3:29), Our Lord's rejoicing in the Holy Spirit (Lk 10:21), Our Lord's promise of joy to His apostles at the Last Supper (Jn 15-16), and the disciples' joy at the Resurrection. Pope Francis went on to point to instances of joy amid suffering and persecution in the Acts of the Apostles, with the conclusion, "Why should we not also enter into this great stream of joy?" (#5, p. 11). This Gospel joy is not separated from emptiness, poverty, and suffering of all sorts. Pope Francis asserted, "I can say that the most beautiful and natural expressions of joy which I have seen in my life were in poor people who had little to hold on to. I also think of the real joy shown by others who, even amid pressing professional obligations, were able to preserve, in detachment and simplicity, a heart full of faith. In their own way, all these instances of joy flow from the infinite love of God, who has revealed himself to us in Jesus Christ" (#7, pp. 11-12).

Near the end of the document, in the final chapter, "Spirit-filled Evangelizers," Pope Francis addressed the joy that needs to accompany the "new evangelization." He explained, "Whenever we say that something is 'spirited,' it usually refers to some interior impulse which encourages, motivates, nourishes and gives meaning to our individual and communal activity. Spirit-filled evangelization is not the same as a set of tasks dutifully carried out despite one's own personal inclinations and wishes. How I long to find the right words to stir up enthusiasm for a new chapter of evangelization full of fervour, joy, generosity, courage, boundless love and attraction! Yet I realize that no words of encouragement will be enough unless the fire of the Holy Spirit burns in our hearts" (*EG*, #261, p. 190). This evangelization, the pope said, must be based on a solid life of prayer and the joy that comes from prayer. He warned, "Without prolonged moments of adoration, of prayerful encounter with the word, of sincere conversation with the Lord, our work easily becomes meaningless; we lose energy as a result of weariness and difficulties, and our fervour dies out. The Church urgently needs the deep breath of prayer, and to my great joy groups devoted to prayer and intercession, the prayerful reading of God's word and the perpetual adoration of the Eucharist are growing at every level of ecclesial life" (*EG*, #262, p. 191). Referring to the joy of the early Church and of saints throughout the ages, the Holy Father reminded us that the joy of being united with Christ and of proclaiming Christ does not depend on an atmosphere of earthly comfort. He asserted, "We do well to keep in mind the early Christians and our many brothers and sisters throughout history who were filled with joy, unflagging courage and zeal in proclaiming the Gospel. Some people nowadays console themselves by saying that things are not as easy as they used to be, yet we know that the Roman empire was not conducive to the Gospel message, the struggle for justice, or the defence of human dignity. Every period of history is marked by the presence of human weakness, self-absorption, complacency and selfishness, to say nothing of the concupiscence which preys upon us all. ... Let us not say, then, that things are harder today; they are simply different. But let us learn also from the saints who have gone before us, who confronted the difficulties of their own day" (*EG*, #263, p. 192). In other words, there is no excuse for not embracing the joy of knowing and loving Christ deeply or for not proclaiming Him with joy!

Pope Francis closed his exhortation with reference to the Blessed Mother, who maintained a spirit of joy despite "moments of aridity, darkness and even fatigue" (*EG*, #287, p. 210). The document ends with a prayer to Mary, including the words, "Filled with Christ's presence, you brought joy to John the Baptist, making him exult in the womb of his mother. Brimming over with joy, you sang of the great things done by God. Standing at the foot of the cross with unyielding faith, you received the joyful comfort of the resurrection, and joined the disciples in awaiting the Spirit so that the evangelizing Church might be born. ... Star of the new evangelization, help us to bear radiant witness to communion, service, ardent and generous faith, justice and love of the poor, that the joy of the Gospel may reach to the ends of the earth, illuminating even the fringes of our world" (*EG*, #288, pp. 211-212). Through the intercession of our Blessed Mother, may we also find joy in this mission to evangelize, which is assigned to all of us in various ways. Then we shall realize that the more we offer to others the joy of the Gospel, the more joy we shall possess in every way and the more joy we shall impart to others.

CHAPTER 8

Applying the *Rule*
and More Recent Texts
to Discover "Lenten Joy"

As an "eschatological gift" that is always available, Christian joy must characterize the life of all Christians, and therefore also of monks, Oblates of St. Benedict, and others who use the *Holy Rule* as a guide. How, in particular, can those who adhere to the *Rule* of St. Benedict open themselves to this joy? How can the application of Benedictine principles enhance one's experiences of Christian joy?

In *RB* 2:30-40, St. Benedict sternly cautions the abbot about his responsibility to direct souls and serve a variety of temperaments. Indeed his task is seen as "a difficult and demanding burden" (*RB* 2:31); he must resist inclinations to have too much concern for temporal things and be "fearful of the future examination" that he will undergo at the Last Judgment. However, there is Christian joy even amid the very awesome nature of the abbot's duties. There is joy in the opportunity to care for souls. There is joy in refocusing one's priorities on the Kingdom of God and learning again and again that "those who fear [God] lack nothing" (*RB* 2:36). There is joy in the opportunity to be especially concerned about one's own relationship with the Lord and to realize that in helping others to amend by warnings, the abbot "achieves the amendment of his own faults" (*RB* 2:40). Thus also for any Christian in a position of authority, the wisdom of the *Rule* for abbots shows that the exercise of authority provides joyful opportunities, not for gain of power or material advantages but for advancing the Kingdom of God, nurturing others' spiritual progress, and finding many occasions to work on one's own faults, which so easily become manifest in the ups and downs of serving as a Christian leader. If an abbot or other authority genuinely cares for those in his charge and adapts himself lovingly to each one's gifts and weaknesses, then he may be able to "rejoice in the increase of a good flock" (*RB* 2:32).

Chapter 3 of the *Rule* tells the abbot that he should consult with the whole community when important business is at hand. St. Benedict reminds the community that they should listen to the younger members since "the Lord often reveals what is better to the younger" (*RB* 3:3). Also, the brothers are urged "to express their opinions with all humility, and not to presume to defend their own views obstinately" (*RB* 3:4). There is joy here, too. It may not be naturally appealing to us to consult with others, especially those who are junior to us. We may be inclined to defend our own opinions and to scheme, however subtly, to have our own views prevail in a group. However, on a Christian level it is a joy to listen to the Lord, wherever and whenever He may speak. It is a joy to bear calmly with the expression of opposite opinions since it offers the occasion for growth in patience. It is a joy to let go of our own will and to embrace God's will, even if the experience is not to our liking and even if the result goes against our preferences. This joy could apply to any gathering. Rather than moan and groan about people whom we find difficult or about not being able to get our way, we can rejoice in our grace-filled capacity to accept others as they are and to bear graciously with decisions that go against our desires. Even the "worst" of meetings can result in our experience of oneness with Christ in His ministry and in His passion. He so often did not get His way with the crowds or with His disciples, not to speak of His enemies and persecutors. If we find genuine joy in preferring "nothing whatever to Christ" (*RB* 72:11) and in being conformed to Him, then this same joy is available even in dealing with a not-so-congenial group of people and even in sitting through the most boring or the most stormy of meetings.

Even the process of dealing with faults and with wayward brothers can be an occasion for joy, mingled though it be with great sadness. In *RB* 28 the community is contending with a brother who fails to amend after frequent reproofs and after the abbot's application of increasingly drastic measures. If the brother reforms, then one has the joy of saving a soul. If all earlier efforts fail, then there is the joy of praying for the brother and putting the whole matter into God's hands. Even if prayers do not produce healing and if the unrepentant brother must be expelled, there is the joy of seeking to prevent the infecting of the whole flock. At each step, even while one grieves over the stubborn waywardness of a fellow Christian, there is a joyful opportunity to cooperate with God's grace to assist a fellow Christian to overcome his dysfunctional behavior; there is an opportunity to cooperate with God's grace to love the wayward one, possibly to witness his healing, and to promote the good of the whole community through the cross of patient efforts to bring about hoped-for reform, whether these measures succeed or fail.

Thus one who seeks to observe the *Holy Rule* can discover its hidden riches by searching for Christian joy in practically every passage. This joy comes not from satisfaction with human achievement or delight in favorable outcomes but from the redeeming involvement of Christ in every situation and in His faithful striving to draw us into His peace, joy and love, even under the most adverse of circumstances.

The reflections on Christian joy in classic and contemporary spiritual literature can also enhance one's understanding of such joy in relationship to discipline, detachment, trials, and growth in hope. The following examples seem, in particular, to highlight themes found in the *Holy Rule*. Evelyn Underhill links Christian joy with the virtue of humility. In her book *Ways of the Spirit*, she asserts, "[J]oy is the mark of perfect consecration, the mysterious result of that complete surrender and death of self which is sanctity. Joy is not a luxury; it is the duty of the soul....It is the sense of our own comparative insignificance as against God's transcendent greatness and perfection....Love makes us humble, and humility makes us joyful....As we get tinier and tinier, everything else gets more majestic and awesome. All sorts of simple things take on a new interest and radiance" (*WS*, p. 65). Thus humble recognition of one's own helplessness can free one from anxious efforts to achieve "great things" on one's own and can liberate one for delight in allowing God to work in His own time and His own way. "Christian joy ... is a grace that comes from God, a grace that irradiates us when we cease to resist in any way His action upon our souls" (*WS*, p. 66).

Joy arises also from progress in "monastic mindfulness" – learning to recognize the hand of God in all things, perhaps especially in difficult situations. According to Brant Pelphrey, in his book *Julian of Norwich*, the mystic Julian proclaimed this sort of joy in her revelations. Pelphrey writes, "The soul who loves God and trusts in the kindness of God learns to recognize God at work in everything. Such a soul stops complaining about suffering and failures and sins, and turns her attention instead to the joy and goodness of God. She enjoys the immediate presence of God, and enjoys God in all things" (*JN*, p. 209). Julian herself discovered such joy amid the great trial of her near-death experience. Furthermore, she proclaimed this joy in an era which suffered from the Black Plague, widespread corruption in Church and state, and the devastation of the Hundred Years' War between France and England. According to Julian, this joy is intimately connected with the redemptive work of Christ. In fact, it is a very share in the joy that God experiences in suffering for us. "The greatest joy in God," she contended, "is not merely in creating and sharing humanity, but in suffering for the sake of humanity; for true joy is compassionate, and true compassion is ultimately always joyful" (*JN*, p. 210). Pelphrey also quotes Julian in her recording of Christ's words to her, proclaiming His joy in His deliberate choice to suffer for our sake out of compassion:

> It is a joy, a blessing and an endless delight to me
> that I ever suffered the passion for you. And if I could
> suffer more, I would suffer more" (*JN*, p. 211, quoting
> Chapter 22 from Julian's *Revelations*).

The joy experienced and proclaimed by Julian also involves a healthy detachment from earthly joys, an overcoming of fear, a refraining from murmuring, and an avoidance of blame. True joy is attained, Julian says, only when we learn to love all that God loves and, therefore, when we "cease to blame God, others, or ourselves for what we perceive as failures in this life" (*JN*, p. 217). The state of pure joy is linked with being "completely at peace, and in love" (*JN*, p. 217, quoting Chapter 49 of *Revelations*). This joy in God grows as we learn to hope in God and not to trust in ourselves even while we see how incomplete we are; thus "the emotion of fear begins to shrink and hope grows" (*JN*, p. 219). Also, "Julian's experience of peace and hope and joy renders her unmoved to gladness by specific things" because "in the light of her visions of Christ as the center of all things, she learns not to take anything in this world as ultimately significant" (*JN*, p. 220). This does not mean total detachment from all things but "an engagement with everything in this world, loving it as God loves it" (*JN*, p. 220). The joyful vision of God's grace in all things overcomes tendencies to murmur and complain, even over evils, since in Christ whatever evil we experience is headed for defeat. Julian goes so far as to say, "I understood that we should laugh in order to comfort ourselves and to enjoy God, because the devil has been overcome" (*JN*, p. 213, quoting Chapter 13 of *Revelations*).

Sister Ruth Burrows speaks of an "invulnerable joy" that we can possess even when we feel abandoned by God. Reflecting on the spirituality of St. John of the Cross in her book *Ascent to Love*, she asserts, "The true signs of the Spirit are very different [from what we experience on the emotional and psychic levels]: an ever-growing selflessness in daily living, self-disregard in all spheres, humility, service, devotedness, and in the inmost heart a joy at being empty of all, poor, abandoned to God as he appears at every moment in whatever guise, able to recognize him when all the senses cry out that this is not he, this could not be he. It is just there that the pure heart sees the humbled face of love that never commands assent but will only ask and invite. The 'joy' in question here is not an emotion; it is a *choosing* to place one's happiness where it properly belongs: in the fulfillment of life's deepest purposes, which is only another way of saying 'pleasing the Father'. This joy is invulnerable. It may be accompanied at times by felt joy, it may not. Either way does not matter. This is Jesus' own joy that nothing can take from us" (*AL*, p. 88). Sister Ruth further points out that St. Thérèse of Lisieux experienced and proclaimed this invulnerable joy amid her own dark experiences. "She said over and over again that she was positively happy to experience her weakness and wretchedness, and she taught her novices to do the same" (*AL*, p. 89). Trust in God and not in her own feelings and inclinations led St. Thérèse to teach, "'Love your weakness. You will gain more by this than if, sustained by grace, you carried off heroic deeds which would foster self-satisfaction and pride'...; in fact, she urged her sisters to pray, 'My God, I'm happy that I have no fine elevated feelings, but I'm glad others have them'" (*AL*, p. 89). What true gladness and joy come from total self-surrender to God and seeking to please Him in all things as opposed to being trapped in self-centered desires!

In his commentary on the *Rule* entitled *The Way to God*, Abbot Emmanuel Heufelder, O.S.B., indicates that "throughout the Holy Rule there is an echo of the Christian joy which the apostle [Paul] wanted to see in those redeemed by Christ" (*WG*, p. 128). Reflecting on the tenth degree of humility, which warns the monk against being "given to ready laughter" (*RB* 7:59), Fr. Emmanuel comments that "Benedict never intended to banish joy from the monastery with this degree" (*WG*, p. 128). Rather, St. Benedict is strongly opposed to an "evil laughter" which is connected with frivolity, unrestrained exuberance, and mere earthly merriment without deeper content, all of which are opposed to true Christian joy. Instead, the tenth degree of humility sets us free "for laughter in humility, for genuine cheerfulness in obedience, for the joy of the Holy Spirit which derives from childlike security in God, from awareness of being sustained by God, and is a foretaste of the never-ending bliss of eternal life" (WG, p. 129). This joy in humility is not opposed to a certain "religious gravity," which is connected with "compunction of heart" and the "tears and sighs" with which we should daily confess our past sins (cf. *RB* 4:2, 52). True Christian joy, says Heufelder, arises from a "holy sorrow" that is related to the second Beatitude and which is required for the attainment of spiritual freedom. Abbot Emmanuel further comments that the road to joyous simplicity is one which results from "long development and effort and only by the grace of God. The *Holy Rule's* degrees of humility embody this long way of development and effort whereby with the help of grace we attain genuine Christian joyfulness" (*WG*, p. 129).

Since joy is such a pervasive theme of Christian life and of the *Rule*, one might do well to meditate on various sections of the *Rule* with the notion of joy in mind and with an inner question, "How am I to find joy here?" As stated above, notions of joy appear chiefly in the Prologue and *RB* 4, 5, 7, and 72; but joy can also be inferred in all the values and practices of the *Rule*. For example, as stated above, one can find joy in silence, which frees the disciple from the demand of frequent talking and the impulse to gain others' attention and esteem. Since the disciple is to be silent and listen (*RB* 6:6), he or she becomes freer to listen to the Lord, to reflect on God's will, to engage in sustained *lectio*, and thus to rejoice that one is able to hear God's voice. God speaks to each one of us in so many varied ways. There is Christian joy in Christian silence.

St. Teresa of Calcutta also lived and proclaimed a Gospel of joy amid a life of prayerful self-discipline and of sacrifices connected with living among the destitute. In the book *Total Surrender* Mother Teresa's instructions include many passages on joyful self-offering. At one point she meditates on joy as follows.

> Joy is indeed the fruit of the Holy Spirit and a
> characteristic mark of the kingdom of God, for God is
> Joy.
>
> Christ wanted to share his joy with his apostles 'That
> my joy may be in you, and that your joy may be full' (Jn
> 15:11).
>
> Joy is prayer,
> - the sign of our generosity, selflessness, and close and
> continual union with God.
>
> Joy is love,

- a joyful heart is the normal result of a heart burning
with love, for she gives most who gives with joy, and
God loves a cheerful giver.

Joy is a net of love by which we can catch souls,
- a sister filled with joy preaches without preaching. Joy
is a need and a power for us even physically, for it makes
us always ready to go about doing good.

The joy of the Lord is our strength (*TS*, p. 42).

Later she adds, "With Jesus our Savior, 'the Lamb led to the
slaughter,' and with our poor, we will accept cheerfully and in the
spirit of faith, all the opportunities He makes especially for us—those
of misunderstanding, of being looked down on, of failure, disgrace,
blame, lack of virtue, and correction. Like Jesus, who submitted
himself to the common law of labor and the common lot of the poor,
we will not seek any special privileges or treatment for ourselves, but
be happy to be treated as one of the poor, ready to be insulted, ill-
treated, refused, blamed falsely, or put to all kinds of inconveniences.
We shall not seek to defend ourselves but leave our defense to the
Lord" (*TS*, p. 43).

Mother Teresa continues, "Cheerfulness is often a cloak which hides
a life of sacrifice, continual union with God, fervor, and generosity.
Joy is one of the most essential things in our Society [Missionaries
of Charity].... Living in the presence of God fills us with joy. God is
joy. To bring joy to us, Jesus became man. Mary was the first one to
receive Jesus: 'My spirit rejoices in God my Savior.'...Joy was also the
characteristic mark of the first Christians. During the persecution,
people used to look for those who had this joy radiating on their
faces. By that joy, they knew who the Christians were, and thus they
persecuted them. St. Paul, whom we are trying to imitate in our zeal,
was an apostle of joy. He urged the early Christians to rejoice in the

Lord always.... Joy is love, the normal result of a heart burning with love. Our lamp will be burning with sacrifices made out of love if we have joy" (*TS*, p. 44-45).

Mother Teresa's Missionaries of Charity are to live in joyful obedience as part of their self-surrender to God and self-sacrificing service to the poor. "Obedience well-lived frees us from selfishness and pride, and so it helps us to find God and, in Him, the whole world. Obedience is a special grace, and it produces unfailing peace, inward joy, and close union with God. ... Obedience lived with joy creates a living awareness of the presence of God, and so fidelity to acts of obedience become like drops of oil that keep the light of Jesus aflame in our life" (*TS*, p. 80).

This joy proclaimed so frequently by St. Teresa of Calcutta is especially remarkable in light of her long experience of inner darkness, which is described in the book *Come Be My Light*, a collection of Mother Teresa's letters edited by Fr. Brian Kolodiejchuk, M.C., with his commentary. Paradoxically, through her experience of distance from God, she became ever closer to Him and grew in her capacity to radiate joy to others. The same can be said for all of us in our experiences of darkness if we learn, in faith, to surrender our darkness, and indeed our whole beings, to God and to His plan for us. Fr. Kolodiejchuk writes, "Mother Teresa accepted all the interior and exterior sufferings God gave her as a privilege, using them to fulfill the aim of her congregation. Yet it was not with a sense of helplessness or passive resignation that she lived; rather she radiated the joy of belonging to God, of living with Him. She knew that after the pain of the Passion, the joy of the resurrection would dawn" (*CBL*, p. 325). Further on, Fr. Kolodiejchuk elaborates on one of her favorite phrases, "something beautiful for God." He states that "it [her use of that motto] was how she had been attempting to show her love for Jesus all these years, doing everything as beautifully as she possibly could for Him. She considered embracing the mystery of the cross in her life an opportunity to do something beautiful for God and carry His love to those living in darkness" (*CBL*, p. 325). He then quotes an exhortation from the saint in a letter to one of her Co-workers: "'In this time of Lent, the time of greater love, when we look at all that Jesus chose to suffer out of love for us, to redeem us, let us pray for all the grace we need to unite our sufferings to His, that many souls, who live in darkness and misery, may know His love and life. ... May Our Lady be a mother to you and help you to stand beneath the Cross with great love. I pray that nothing may ever so fill you with pain and sorrow as to make you forget the joy of the Risen Jesus" (*CBL*, pp. 325-326).

Are we not all to become living sacrifices of praise, seeking an ever fuller self-surrender to God in love? Are not Benedictine vowed religious, Oblates of Saint Benedict, and others who find wisdom in the *Holy Rule* especially committed to a "monastic mindfulness" that nurtures a living awareness of God's presence and a life continually aflame with the light of Jesus? Then let us strive to live in joyful obedience from moment to moment as did Mother St. Teresa and all the saints.

CHAPTER 9

Actual Experiences of Finding Joy in Everyday Life, Even in Distress

Ways for all of us to enter into Christian joy

In his doctoral research, Fr Kurt found in the Vulgate Bible four categories of joy combined with suffering: joy and discipline, joy and sacrifice *per se*, joy and trials in general, and joy in suffering persecution. All of these are related to instances of joy found in the *Holy Rule*. St. Benedict's use of "with the joy of the Holy Spirit" (*RB* 49:6) is directly related to the themes of joy in suffering, joy in hope, and joy in asceticism found in St. Paul's letters. (The *Rule's* phrase probably comes directly from 1 Thes 1:16, which reads, "And you became imitators of us and of the Lord, receiving the word in great affliction, with joy from the Holy Spirit.") Fr. Kurt sees St. Benedict's summons to joy in Lent connected to four themes of Benedictine life and spirituality: (1) monastic life as a dynamic process of maturity in the Spirit taking time, (2) the practices or observances which help one to arrive at this maturity, (3) the spiritual freedom that is accessible through obedience to those whose wills and desires are transformed by the Holy Spirit, and (4) an unconditional preference for and surrender to Christ. How can we find joy in these realms in our daily lives as Christians who have come to know the *Rule* of St. Benedict?

First of all, perhaps it should be stated that joy should be found in situations that bring us obvious blessings. In our suspicious, cynical age some of us may be inclined not to rejoice in "natural joys" because they are not lasting, because sorrow is likely to follow soon, because those who cause us joy may have unperceived ulterior motives, or because we see ourselves unworthy to receive such blessings. Our faith tells us, however, that we should rejoice in obvious blessings, even if they are mixed with other undesirable elements, because they are ultimately gifts from our loving God, and even the unredeemed phenomena connected with these blessings provide opportunities to welcome Christ's redeeming love.

Therefore, we should learn to rejoice in the Lord when we witness bodily healing in ourselves or others. We should rejoice in manifest signs of unselfish human love. We should rejoice in reconciliation between once-estranged people and in peace agreements between groups of people. We should rejoice in generous bestowals of material gifts. We should rejoice when, by God's grace, we see people overcoming hunger, oppression, poverty, misery, or injustice of any kind. We should rejoice when our prayer is deeply consoling. (That may be a rare phenomenon for some of us!) We should rejoice when we observe others enjoying a honeymoon of Christian conversion or any spiritual consolation.

On the other hand, the greater challenge is to find joy in situations of personal sacrifice and discipline and occasions of external trials. It is these that test and stretch our Christian faith and teach us not to lose hope but rather to be drawn to greater loving self-surrender to Christ. This notion of joy does not mean, of course, that we somehow "enjoy" the suffering involved; that would be masochism, a disorder. Instead, we can learn to discover and appreciate the presence of Christ amid our suffering, the graces for spiritual growth He is giving us through the suffering, and the opportunity for deeper communion with Him and with others who suffer in similar ways. Thus the suffering becomes an occasion to have our hearts expanded in love.

Joy in prayer and fasting

We can find joy when prayer is difficult for us. If we ourselves have been negligent, then we can welcome the grace of repentance and reorder our priorities to give proper place to prayer in our lives. If we have not been particularly negligent, then we can rejoice that in being deprived of self-satisfaction we are reminded that we are at prayer to please the Lord rather than to please ourselves. We can rejoice that God gives us grace to persevere in prayer even if we do not feel good about it. If possible, we can decide to extend our dry prayer by some minutes and rejoice that God does appreciate our every effort not to lose hope but to trust that He supports us in love amid our poverty and emptiness. Even if we have no words but only "tears of compunction" (RB 20:3), we can rejoice that God is filling our emptiness with His own hidden presence and is helping us to gain greater purity of heart.

Regarding the Divine Office, we can rejoice that the Church has given us a set form of prayer that unites us with Christ and the rest of the Church in heaven and on earth. We can rejoice that others, perhaps people whom we know, are drawn to pray the Liturgy of the Hours and thus to strengthen our own resolution. We can rejoice that God has given us the psalms that enable us to pray with His own words whether or not we ourselves as individuals can generate harmonizing thoughts and feelings. We can rejoice in the graces of the discipline that the Lord gives us to pray the Office as much as our schedules allow, whether or not we always accept those graces. We can rejoice in the struggle to keep our minds in harmony with our voices (*RB* 19:7), both of which Christ uses to help us to work and pray in deeper union with Him. We can rejoice even when we do not share in the sentiments of a given psalm because we can then pray with and for someone else who *can* identify with the sentiments, so that the Lord may expand our hearts to be more closely united with others for whom we might not otherwise care. Finally, we can rejoice that if we pray the Office faithfully, we shall some day pray with greater joy and zeal as it becomes part of our lives; in fact, if we persevere until death, we can rejoice in the firm hope that we shall be praying a greatly transformed form of the Office in the fullness of joy with the angels and saints in heaven.

We can rejoice in opportunities to practice fasting (*RB* 49:7, 4:13). (In fact, there is a book entitled *To Love Fasting*, based on the verse *RB* 4:13.) We can rejoice in the grace not to give in to selfish indulgence but rather to "empty ourselves" of gluttonous tendencies for the Lord. We can rejoice that the practice of eating only what we really need (or sometimes even less) can unite us with others who suffer from chronic hunger, especially if we can donate the money saved to alleviate world hunger. If we find ourselves craving food, we can rejoice that the Lord is revealing to us how weak and how dependent on food we are and how we need Him to transform our cravings into a far better hunger—the lasting hunger for salvation in Christ and for Christ Himself, who is our true joy. We can rejoice if fasting sets us free from unhealthy patterns of eating (as it should) and helps us to turn to Christ, rather than "creature comforts," to fill our inner emptiness.

Joy in the practice of sacrificial love

We can rejoice if we are called to sacrifice our time and energy for others, especially when we feel deprived of our own agenda and our own preferences. We can rejoice in the opportunity to let God's plan replace our plans. We can rejoice in the grace to overcome murmuring and, if we tend to be chronic murmurers, in the realization that we need persistent prayer and custody over our thoughts and words to remedy such a fault—and that God's grace will surely assist us in this endeavor. We can rejoice in the call to serve Christ in other persons, particularly if the persons are those whom we might not really feel like helping. In being called away from our projects, we can rejoice in the assurance that we are more likely to be working to build up the Kingdom when God has chosen our course of action through our being interupted by others. God's choice of such "penances," which help us to achieve true repentance where we need it most, are always better than the penances that we ourselves might choose during Lent! If we succeed in immediately "[putting] aside [our] own concerns" (*RB* 5:7) to respond quickly to a summons, we can rejoice in the grace that helped us to obey. If, on the other hand, our obedience was "cringing or sluggish or half-hearted" (*RB* 5:14) or grudging, we can rejoice that God uses our reaction of unwillingness to humble us and show us how far we have yet to go in developing the virtue of obedience. We can rejoice in the hope that if we keep trying to obey promptly, God will draw us towards "unhesitating obedience, which comes naturally to those who cherish Christ above all" (*RB* 5:1-2). Our very failures to prefer Christ and His will over our wills can give us an incentive to cooperate with ever-available graces to become a cheerful giver in surrendering ourselves with and in Christ.

Joy in humility and in occasions of uncertainty

We can rejoice in the opportunity to grow in humility when we do not know how to respond to a given situation. We can rejoice in the truth of our own ignorance and our need to rely on God and others to show the way. If we are tempted to "plead lack of resources as an excuse" (*RB* 2:35) to escape from a duty to which we have been called, we can rejoice, like the abbot in *RB* 2, that God will provide all that we need if only we seek His Kingdom first (2:35). If we are dealing with other people, then we can rejoice that our lack of a ready solution prevents us from imposing our own cherished notions on those who are different from us; our acknowledged helplessness can motivate us to serve people's real needs and to regard them as persons whose sorrows we are to share rather than as problematic individuals whom we might prefer to ignore. We can rejoice that indecision and frustration over our inadequacy can help us to surrender situations to God and to listen for every subtle sign of His guidance, even as we proceed to do our feeble best to fulfill a given duty.

Rejoicing in dealing with difficult or hostile people

We can rejoice amid the trial of bearing someone's burdens, even when we feel naturally annoyed by that person's faults or weaknesses (cf. *RB* 72:5). We can rejoice in being stretched in patience. If, for example, someone is groaning to us about minor ailments, we can, in faith, see an opportunity to love by listening and by praying for healing of the far deeper hurts that probably underlie the verbalized aches and pains. We can rejoice in the grace to resist condemning (and I must plead for that grace relentlessly in some situations!) and to divert our energy to a prayerful appeal for our mutual conversion in Christ's love. Perhaps we can rejoice, too, that prayerful reflection reveals that we also have tendencies to grumble about certain matters and that the negative example of others can strengthen our resolve not to fall into the same pit. Finally, we can rejoice that such little "persecutions" can lead us to fuller possession of the Kingdom in heaven since they lead us to be conformed to Christ in His own sufferings (Mt 5:10, 11).

We can rejoice, too, in the more genuine persecution of being treated unjustly (cf. *RB* 7:35). If it is someone else or a group who are suffering injustice, then we may be called to work to establish peace and justice by whatever means the Lord has given. However, if it is we who are suffering and if (as so often is the case) there is no way to remove the unjust condition in a morally Christian way, then we must quietly embrace the suffering and rejoice in the grace to endure "without weakening or seeking escape" (*RB* 7:36). We can rejoice that we must rely on the Lord in order to bear courageously with the injustice. We can rejoice that our practice of patient endurance is sort of "death" experienced in union with Christ, the Lamb led to slaughter (cf. *RB* 7:38). We can rejoice in letting go of our understandably human hopes for release from the challenge and in embracing the present and future "reward" that comes from God, the present gift being His compassionate, if unfelt, presence even here and now. We can rejoice, too, that being supported by Christ who loves us, we can strive to love those who are responsible for the injustice. We can rejoice in being able to "bless those who curse" (*RB* 7:43) us and thus open the way to the redemptive love offered to us by Christ to extend to our persecutors.

Joy in good zeal: the call to obey the needs of others and bear with the weaknesses of others

The good zeal of *RB* 72 could be interpreted as living joyfully amid non-ideal conditions for the sake of Christ. *RB* 71 embodies similar themes. Although obedience to others, whether to our superiors or to our equals, can be trying, it is a genuine blessing "since we know that it is by this way of obedience that we go to God" (*RB* 71:2). We can rejoice in occasions to show love and concern in obedience to our elders, even though their requests or their manner of approach may irritate us; with faith we can learn that their flaws need to be healed by love and can be healed only by love. When someone reproves us, whether rightly or not, we can rejoice in taking the initiative to admit our imperfections and thus to seek reconciliation, although, of course, we are not bound to accept blame when we are not at fault (cf. *RB* 71:6-8).

Likewise, we can rejoice in the good zeal that urges us to respect others even when they seem not to be respecting us (*RB* 72:4). In Christ, we must not fear humbling ourselves or being put down; if we are not treated as we wish, all the more reason to rejoice! We can rejoice not only in putting up with others' weaknesses but in supporting others in their limitations with love and the greatest patience (*RB* 72:5). (The Latin word for this expresses its beauty: *patientissime!*) We can rejoice in "competing" in the only competition that makes Christian sense: the "winning" that comes from heeding and obeying others even when they seem not to appreciate us (*RB* 72:6). We can rejoice in the grace to pursue what is better for others rather than for ourselves, for this capacity in a major test of Christian love (cf. *RB* 72:7). In our ongoing pilgrimage of learning to "prefer nothing whatever to Christ" (*RB* 72:11), we can find joy in all sorts of things that would otherwise cause us dismay; for the very difficulties that we are called to endure become stepping stones to a deeper communion with Christ and to the expansion of our all-too-narrow hearts in His love. It is through trials that we learn to love our family members, friends, neighbors, and co-workers; it is through trials that we learn to love our superiors, whether civil or religious, in a humble, unfeigned way (cf. *RB* 72:10). It is through trials that we learn the "loving fear" (*RB* 72:9) of God, who challenges us to transcend our very limited earthly hopes and desires. It is through learning to rejoice in trials for the sake of Christ that, in our own small way, we, in communion with Christ, contribute to "bring[ing] us all together to everlasting life" (*RB* 72:12).

Joy in dealing with our own illnesses

St. Benedict speaks about the special care that sick monks should receive (*RB* 36). Sometimes the Lord Himself brings noticeable blessings when we have inconvenient health problems. I recall having a sinus headache before preaching on a special occasion. In retrospect, I realized that the headache itself brought down upon me graces that I would not have otherwise enjoyed. For one thing, the pain taught me to avoid a certain food. Secondly, the headache dulled my expected nervousness over speaking for an event over which I felt ill at ease and unprepared. Thirdly, because of the pain and my own feelings of inadequacy, I could not get upset over the lamentable lack of organization of the details of the Mass which was involved in the occasion—a disorganization which normally leaves me tense and frustrated. Yes, we can learn much from our own illnesses—compassion for others who are vulnerable, a clearer perspective on life, acknowledgment of our chronic inadequacy, and the availability of overflowing graces. In all this we can rejoice!

Specific instances of discovering joy amid trials

The experience of tragic death

One of the most traumatic experiences of my childhood was the sudden death of my maternal grandfather when I was six years old. Even though he had pneumonia and was worn out from long years of work in a broom factory, his death was rather sudden, and the loss of his presence was shocking to our whole family. It was especially difficult since my parents, who had never known their grandparents, who remained in Lithuania while my four grandparents immigrated to the United States in the early 1900's, had not experienced the death of close loved ones. There was hardly any tangible joy in the months (or perhaps even several years) of mourning for my grandfather, who had shown me great love as his first grandchild.

In retrospect, however, I can see reasons to rejoice. The Lord somehow sustained my grandmother, my mother, and the whole family through this difficult time. In praying for the repose of my grandfather's soul (and even for his possible return) as a second-grader, I learned to enjoy my time with the Lord in the dark of my bedroom after our family had finished the bedtime prayers that we recited together. I learned about the reality and the finality of death. The truths about heaven, hell, and purgatory became deeply embedded in me. Since all of us were faithful to our Catholic obligation to pray for the souls in purgatory, this devotion became an especially important part of my prayer life and remains so to this day. Finally, after having lost almost all of my other family members in the sixty-four years since my maternal grandfather's death, I can experience the anticipatory joy of looking forward to meeting him and my other deceased loved ones—along with the risen Christ—

when it comes time for me to die and complete my time of purgation. What a joyful reunion it will be!

The remembering of kindnesses in times of illness

As a child growing up in the 1950's, I ended up contracting most of the usual childhood diseases—chicken pox, measles, and mumps. (I think that I somehow avoided German measles.) In the days before vaccines for these diseases, one was practically expected to become sick and stay in bed for a few days when the disease started to spread among classmates or siblings. I happened to be ill with measles in February, 1958, when I was in the second grade. I did not enjoy missing school or being confined to bed. However, I vaguely remember the joy of being shown great kindness by my parents and other family members.

I would not even have remembered the date of my having measles if it were not for a discovery that I made in the spring of 2020. In spending free time on Sundays reviewing old letters sent to me in past decades (and I had more spare time than usual during the initial weeks of the coronavirus pandemic), I was intending to unclutter my monastic cell by throwing most of the letters away. Once in a while, I would find a real "gem," which I would save or give to someone who might better appreciate it. The letters, stored alphabetically in boxes by year, were sent to me between 1967 and 2018, when I began the process of clearing them out. In any case, one Sunday I found an unusual item among the letters: an envelope postmarked February, 1958, with a succession of six or seven smaller envelopes inside. Each inner envelope was smaller than the previous one, and each displayed a cartoon character growing impatient with the slow process of getting to the ultimate message. I kept opening the succession of envelopes with the joyful expectation of a child. (I did suspect that the mailing was from my aunt who was also godmother since her address was on the outside.) When I finally opened the last and smallest envelope, I found the beautiful message: get-well wishes from my aunt and uncle, my grandmother, and my cousin. What joy it gave me to think that the item had somehow survived for sixty-two years without being thrown out. It also gave me joy to remember my aunt's great thoughtfulness and then to contact my cousin (her son) whose name was on the card. He indeed wanted me to send it to him so that he could pass it on to his children (if indeed they would want to keep the "ancient" greeting card). It gave me special joy to share the news with him and to send him the precious item. We can only imagine the far greater joy we shall have in heaven when God will help us to remember with gratitude all such occasions of loving kindness bestowed on us in the course of our lives.

The joy and pain of long-range discernment of a vocation

It was probably the inspiring example of Pope Saint John XXIII and the painful news about his dying from cancer in June of 1963 that first motivated me to consider priesthood as a vocation. In the fall of that year, during a Sunday catechism lesson, the religious sister who taught our ninth-grade class spoke about priestly and religious vocations. The thought of becoming a priest brought me some joy at that moment, and I held on to it. In fact, I prayed about openness to the possibility for over eleven years without telling anyone—not even my parents or my pastor, whom I knew rather well, or anyone else. I feared that others would understand my "secret" thoughts or that they would think me foolish or misguided for considering a priestly vocation. The only option that I felt I could choose was to wait in silence and prayer until the time would come, perhaps in my old age, when I could pursue the vocation outwardly.

Well, the time seemed to come in 1973-1975, during my final years in graduate school. Frustrated with my lack of fulfillment in writing a dissertation in applied mathematics and tasting great satisfaction with my weekly volunteer visits to patients in a nursing home, the idea of priestly vocation resurfaced in my heart, and I felt that I needed to find someone trustworthy who would make sense of these stirrings. I finally decided to see a Jesuit priest on campus, a fellow graduate student, who helped with campus-ministry Masses, who celebrated Mass with striking reverence, and who preached convincingly. When I made an appointment with him and went to see him, I felt the pain and the joy of communicating my long-kept secret. The priest did not think me foolish or misguided. Instead, he listened compassionately, responded by saying that I might indeed have a vocation to priesthood and/or religious life, and suggested that I continue to meet with him. Therefore, I did so. As a result of these sessions of spiritual direction, I began inquiries into several religious communities. After the completion of my degree and emergence into the world of work (for an engineering company), I continued my painful but joyful pursuit until the Lord made it rather clear where He wanted me to be. Amid the pain of uncertainty and of fear of upsetting people who might not understand, I discovered the joy of listening to the Lord more intently and of entrusting my future to Him, even as for a long time I did not know where He would direct me. May we all know the joy of discovering the Lord's direction for us after however short or long a time He leaves us in painful uncertainty!

Joy of valuing relationships amid distress

In the spring before my last year of graduate school, there was a lottery to determine which students would live in dormitory rooms on campus and which rooms they would be assigned. Having been at the university for two academic years, I was anticipating having to live off campus, or at best being assigned a less desirable room, since the newer graduate students received better numbers in the lottery, it being assumed that the senior students would be more capable of finding off-campus housing. In any case, weeks went by after the lottery, and I was not notified of my number. Therefore, I went in person to see a staff member at the housing office. When she looked at the lottery listing, she saw that my name had been accidentally omitted. With apologies, she gave me a list of all the rooms still available in the forthcoming semester and said that, in reparation for the office's error, I could choose any room that had not yet been claimed. It turned out that a room right next to the room that I already inhabited was available. What a wonderful surprise! Furthermore, the room was almost twice as large as my current room and yet would not cost any more.

At the end of the summer I easily moved my belongings from one dorm room to the other. The new room needed much cleaning. In order to do a thorough job, I used a special spray to pick up dust, another spray to clean the windows, and then still another aerosol spray to polish the furniture. Then, on top of all those chemicals, I used an air-freshener spray to minimize all the other odors. I did not open the windows since the weather was exceptionally cool. Within a few days after I moved in, I began to have respiratory problems, especially during mornings and evenings. After over a week the congestion did not improve, and I reluctantly considered seeing a doctor.

About that time I was in regular contact with a student who was trying to schedule a Bible study for the fall semester. I was a member of the group, and he wanted to make sure that he had my input before setting a date and time for our weekly meeting. When he phoned me one evening, I was in the midst of a bad coughing fit. He asked me what was the matter. When I told him, he came to the very logical conclusion that I had somehow missed, namely that perhaps I was reacting to something in the dorm room. I finally realized that it was probably all those aerosol sprays that were giving me an allergic reaction; so I thereupon opened the windows to air out the room, and within a day or two my symptoms ceased.

Pondering the overall meaning of these events, I realized with gratitude and joy that many graces had been involved. God had worked through the employee in the housing office to assign me a very desirable room that I had no reason to expect. My allergic reaction taught me not to rejoice so much in the material benefit of obtaining a desirable room but rather to delight in the generosity with which I had been treated. Finally, I naturally experienced joy over the kindness of the student coordinating the Bible study—and even over my quasi-illness, which turned out to be the cause of unexpected blessings. As expressed by St. Paul in a verse especially treasured by St. Thérèse, "Everything is a grace!" (Rom 4: 16).

Experience of thwarted expectation leading to a joyful discovery of grace

When Holy Week arrived during my novitiate at Saint Vincent Archabbey, I was expecting a deep and emotionally joyful plunge into the Paschal mystery, especially during the Triduum. During the previous two years of strong involvement in my parish in the diocese where I had lived, I had had a taste of the beauty of the liturgies of

Holy Thursday through Easter Sunday, and I was hoping for an even more thrilling experience at the monastery. Well, my hopes turned out to be largely dashed. When Holy Week arrived, I learned that we novices were expected to perform all sorts of extra work. Since we were to serve at all the great liturgies, there were many practice sessions for these ceremonies. We also were assigned to help to clean the many sacred vessels in the sacristy. I cannot remember the other extra duties, but I do recall that I viewed all these surprises, sometimes revealed to us on short notice, as burdens that were taking me away from *my* peace and *my* leisure and *my* ability to enjoy the liturgies and the prayerful atmosphere of the Sacred Triduum.

It turned out that God had some additional surprises for me that helped to turn my sour disposition into genuine joy. On Good Friday I was assigned to be one of the servers who held a cross for people to venerate. As I held the precious symbol of God's love for us, I could not help being deeply moved by the expressions on the faces of many of the people who came forward. I could perceive their sense of pain and sorrow mingled with their deep love for Jesus and their appreciation of His death for us. I was practically in tears myself and was genuinely caught up in the mystery of the Passion. How grateful we should all be for the death of Christ! Those moments of holding the cross came to be a treasured highlight of the sacred days.

The other great liturgies of the Triduum were less moving for me. I felt as if I were being dragged from one thing to another without being able to catch much breath in-between. At the end of the Triduum, on the evening of Easter Sunday after a festive meal, I felt totally exhausted; but there was still a scheduled evening social for the monastic community. Out of obedience, I attended it although what I really wanted to do was to go straight to bed. In the course of the hour-long event, I found myself in the presence of another young but very wise monk. He thoughtfully asked me how I had experienced Holy Week and the Triduum. Appreciating his show of concern, I bared my soul to him and told him how my expectations had been thwarted and how I had felt loss of control over my life for several days. At the end of my mournful discourse, he gently paused and then said to me, "Was not your experience of suffering a share in Christ's Passion?" It did not take me long to realize that his assessment of my situation was absolutely correct. All that disappointment and loss of control was very much a part of what Our Lord was suffering in His Passion, and that realization gave me a new perspective on the whole week, a glimpse of how God had been working in me through all the apparent chaos, and a sense of joy that I had been brought closer to the Lord Jesus in my seemingly negative experience.

The next morning at breakfast, I happened to be sitting next to a compassionate senior monk, who unexpectedly asked me, "What was your resurrection experience these past few days?" How amazing! I then recounted to him the details of my ordeal and the grace-filled encounter at the evening social. We then were able to smile and laugh together, and having verbalized the "conversion experience" to someone who understood, I was able to rejoice all the more. My experience was akin to that of the two disciples on the way to Emmaus; I encountered the risen Lord not just once but in the two monks with whom I shared my "Passion story."

Unexpected joys from surrendering to others' preferences

As my two Benedictine seminary classmates and I prepared for ordination to the priesthood, both of them wanted to make a retreat at a Trappist monastery. I did not want to go that far away and preferred to go to near-by St. Emma Monastery or to our monastery's "Ridge house." However, I went along with their majority opinion, and they obtained our abbot's permission for having our retreat at an unprecedented location; so off we went to a place of much silence and solitude, from a Monday to a Friday.

Besides the burden of driving some five hours, we Benedictines were told that we could not live in the monastery but had to stay in the guest house, where lay retreatants were also staying. We also had our meals in the guest-house dining room. Those limitations were a disappointment to me. However, we three were allowed to join the Trappist monks for Vigils, Lauds, Mass, Vespers, and Compline in their main chapel as long as we wore our habits.

Despite my misgivings, it turned out that I enjoyed the atmosphere of the monastery chapel and the grounds. Not minding going to bed early and rising very early, I enjoyed the mile-or-so walk under starry skies to participate in Vigils at about 2:30 A.M. each morning. In fact, although we were given flashlights to make our way to the monastery in those very early hours, I realized that the light of the stars and the moon were bright enough to illuminate my way. (That seemed like a foretaste of the joy of the Last Day, after which, according to Revelation, we who enter into heaven will need no light from the sun or moon because the Lord Himself will be our light!) I enjoyed the atmosphere in the dark chapel even though I sometimes had a hard time finding my place in the liturgical books. I enjoyed the relatively early Hour of Compline, and especially its ending with the singing of a Marian antiphon with our gaze fixed on a lit-up icon of the Blessed Mother and the child Jesus.

One of the especially tangible blessings of the retreat occurred on the memorial of St. Anselm of Canterbury, a Benedictine saint, when the abbot invited us three Benedictines to have a tour of the monastery and to have lunch with the Trappist monks. That was a special delight. In particular, the simple lunch, eaten in silence to the accompaniment of classical music, was in a dining room which had a huge picture window with a beautiful view of the scene outside. Furthermore, the music, played on an old-fashioned phonograph, was interrupted when the needle became stuck in a groove. Even the Trappist monks started to chuckle when that mishap occurred, and I found joy in that very human dimension of our retreat.

In sum, something that I initially opposed and then accepted reluctantly turned out to be a great blessing for me. Although I was confirmed in my commitment to spend my life as a monk-priest of St. Vincent Archabbey and did not expect to travel to that Trappist monastery again, I hope always to remember the joys that the Lord gave me during those five days as a sign of His ongoing and lavish graces that continue to support me in my vocations as a monk and as a priest.

The joy of finding grace after doing something humanly unreasonable

The vow of obedience, which applies formally to superiors in the monastery, does not exclude continuing obedient listening to family and friends—or to fellow monks or anyone else with whom we relate. As I was preparing to send out invitations to my priestly ordination in the spring of 1983, my aunt, who was also my godmother, insisted that I send invitations to cousins in the Chicago and Detroit areas. Since I had never met the cousins in Michigan and since my family had visited the cousins in Chicago only once, in 1965, I thought that it was unreasonable to invite them. I felt sure that they would not come. However, my aunt was very insistent. Therefore, I sent invitations to these cousins; it was worth the extra cost of postage to please my persistent aunt. Then, to my amazement, three cousins from the Chicago area and three from the Detroit area accepted the invitation. When the day before my ordination came, it was a joy to greet them all and to give them (and other guests) tours of the campus of Saint Vincent Archabbey. I had a sense of the "whole world's" being present at my ordination; there they were, a mixture of family, friends, and monks who got to meet one another for the first time. Perhaps it was a little taste of heaven. Beyond the occasion of the ordination (and Masses of thanksgiving that many of these people were able to attend), an ongoing relationship developed with my distant cousins, and I have kept up correspondence with them for decades. The joy was multiplied in recent years when I found it important to travel to Ann Arbor, Michigan, for a friend's profession of religious vows. Although I dislike traveling such distances and spending substantial time away from the Archabbey, those two trips gave me opportunities to visit some of the cousins in the Detroit area; in the case of three cousins, the visits became especially precious because they died within a few years after my visits; so I can look forward to a reunion with them in heaven all the more since I enjoyed valuable encounters with them here on earth.

All these blessings stemmed from my reluctant obedience to my insistent aunt, who possessed some wisdom, especially concerning relationships, that I lacked. I hope that I may continue to find joy in eager obedience to superiors, to fellow monks, and to family members, even when I cannot see the benefits of such obedience. The joy flowing from these occasions arises from the opportunity to conform oneself to Christ in His lifelong obedience to the Father, especially in the surrender of His life. How much more should we, in union with Him, surrender ourselves in situations that are much less painful than His Passion and that sometimes even turn out to be pleasant and rewarding from an earthly perspective.

Discovering joy amid serious illness

In the summer of 1983, two and a half months after my ordination as a priest, I was diagnosed with viral pneumonia after I had experienced about a week of almost incessant coughing, very little sleep, and loss of appetite. When I saw the doctor on his weekly visit to our monastery, he quickly diagnosed me with pneumonia and ordered me to go to the hospital. Up to that point, I had never been ill in the hospital; so having to report to the hospital was a bit humiliating. On the other hand, at first I was just glad to have some hope of relief from the misery that I had felt for over a week. In the hospital I was soon put on an I.V. and given an antibiotic. Within a day I responded with a bad reaction to the antibiotic and felt more ill than I had at the time of admission; so the antibiotic had to be changed. Then, even as I began to improve, more misery was in store. After about three days I became impatient and really wanted to go home to the monastery. Since the time when I was supposed to report to a new assignment was fast approaching, I did not want the additional humiliation of arriving late as parochial vicar of the parish to which the abbot had assigned me. When I complained to a doctor that I should be going home since I felt much better, he told me that I had a nodule on my lung that needed to be further tested; it could be a matter of cancer, tuberculosis, or something else. That was a surprise! Of course, I was a bit frightened, but even then I realized that the Lord might be giving me an opportunity to face death. I was hoping that my life and my priesthood would last a good while longer; but if the Lord chose otherwise, what might seem like a waste from a human perspective might be an opportunity to surrender to God's all-wise, loving plan.

Where was joy in all of this? Certainly there was no felt joy in the misery of being very seriously ill or being diagnosed with a possibly fatal condition. However, as I reflected on my experience, there were many occasions for gratitude and joy even as I lay on a hospital bed. First of all, I was overwhelmed by the kindness shown by so many of my fellow monks. I received many visits from them, and the abbot himself contacted me every day of my hospitalization, either by phone call or by personal visit. The hospital chaplain, who was one of the monks, brought me Holy Communion. An older monk who regularly visited patients as a volunteer came to me even before the regular chaplain and administered the Sacrament of the Anointing of the Sick to me in its full form. At the time I did not fully appreciate the lengthy, elaborate ceremony; but afterwards the image of the priest's coming to me with the sacrament stayed with me and reminded me of his commendable devotion as a monk and priest, even though he was well over eighty years old. I learned to appreciate the skill, kindness, and coordination of the two nurses who were assigned to take care of one of my roommates, who was rather cantankerous but who seemed to become gentler over the course of several days. (I was even able to help him myself in a few small ways since he was elderly and quite disabled.) After a few days I felt well enough to celebrate Mass, and the prior brought a Mass kit to me. What a joy it was for me to celebrate Mass in a simple, humble way on my small bedside table! Even the possible diagnosis with a critical condition like tuberculosis or cancer proved to be a hidden blessing. It forced me to think about death and to recognize the need to keep death in mind daily as St. Benedict urges us to do in *RB* 4:47. Being aware of the possible closeness of death helped me to live focused on Christ through the unwanted illness and to aim for a disposition of praise and thanksgiving, whatever my feelings might be.

Of course, one of the great blessings stemming from my illness was the immense gratitude I felt as my body recovered. It was all gift! When finally I was allowed to report to my parish assignment fifteen days after my hospitalization, I could experience the joy of being a new priest in a parish. In fact, I found special joy in visiting patients in a hospital and a nursing home as part of my ministry. Having been in a hospital bed for a week, I could empathize better with the bedridden patients whom I visited. I could especially understand the frustration that some of them felt when they wanted to leave and go home but were not permitted. Furthermore, I found many patients who turned out to be more or less homebound and who needed someone to bring them Holy Communion monthly. These people ended up being on my list of monthly home visits so that I could experience the joy (and the burden shared with Christ) of bringing the Holy Eucharist to a great number of people on first Fridays, on the Thursdays that preceded, and then even on the Wednesdays that preceded (because there were ultimately too many people to visit on one or even two days). Beyond the joy that I experienced, I could sense the joy that most of these "shut-ins" felt when I came to them with the Our Lord in the Blessed Sacrament. All these blessings emerged from the frustrating phenomenon of being hospitalized with viral pneumonia. May God be praised!

Joy in surrendering one's will and overcoming judgment

One day while I was serving as a parochial vicar at the same parish mentioned above, I was asked on short notice to attend a "renewal workshop" for priests sponsored by the diocese. The event, located in another city, was to last from a Monday until the following Friday and involved overnight accommodations. Feeling overwhelmed with work as I usually did (and still do), I protested that I could not afford to leave five days of work behind. However, I was told to go anyway. Priests from two other Catholic parishes in town were going, and I would ride with them. Of course, I somewhat reluctantly obeyed, undoubtedly with some inner murmuring.

At the first session we participants were introduced to the presenter, a Jesuit priest. He seemed a bit unkempt in his appearance and was smoking a cigarette much of the time. Upon seeing him, I felt even worse about the whole event and did not expect much good from it. However, I soon was attracted by the priest's passionate love for the Church and his desire to set us other priests "on fire" with a similar love. Within a day I was very much caught up in the theme of the workshop, which could be summarized as inspiring people in Catholic parishes to develop a passionate love for Christ and for their Catholic faith. I assiduously took notes and hoped that the ideas mentioned in the presenter's talks could be applied in my parish in some way.

One outcome of the workshop was that our parish in conjunction with another parish in town held several "renewal weekends" led by another priest and me. They were not as well attended as we had hoped, but it seems that the participants were genuinely interested in growing into a deeper faith through these retreats. I cannot forget the positive impact of the whole experience, including acceptance of the limitations of parishioners and of my own eagerness to extend to others the enthusiasm that I originally felt. Perhaps the greatest reason for genuine joy was the fact that I was led to a greater love for the Catholic faith and the Church and that I received graces to let go of my reluctance to do something new and inconvenient, to put aside my prejudices and spontaneous judgment of those who do not fit my expectations, and to embrace the surprises that God has in store, even in the midst of frustrations and disappointments. Furthermore, another somewhat surprising outcome was that shortly after the event for priests, we monks who were stationed in three different parishes began to pray Evening Prayer together on weekdays. That development, too, was a cause for genuine joy.

Joy in learning painfully to appreciate beauty

Some years ago I was blessed to hear a rather well-known Benedictine author as a featured guest speaker at an Oblate directors' meeting in New Jersey. Furthermore, I learned that she was able and willing to give a presentation at St. Vincent Archabbey before she was scheduled to fly to her home. The condition for her spending a day or two at the Archabbey was that, for budgetary reasons, I would need to drive her from the monastery in New Jersey to St. Vincent. I felt honored to be driving this guest for the trip of five hours or so. On the other hand, I was somewhat fearful about anything that might go wrong. During the journey on an expressway in northern Pennsylvania, a strong downpour erupted so that I had to go off the road and wait until it subsided. After that the guest and I were talking so much that I, already shaken by the storm, missed an exit. Then I was even more dismayed; when I took the next exit, I did not know where we were, and we might not even arrive at the Archabbey in time for Vespers. While I was internally fretful and fearful, my guest was marveling at the beautiful scenery. Indeed the scenery *was* beautiful. We were traveling through an area with an abundance of trees and flowering bushes, all glistening from the rain that had fallen. Little by little, I realized that my guest, in expressing her wonder and awe, had a far better disposition than I did. Furthermore, within a short time I noticed a sign that led us to a road with which I was familiar and that would easily lead us to the Archabbey. We did indeed arrive in time for Vespers.

Thus all my fretting was for naught. I am still learning to aspire to appreciate the beauties of God's natural world with joy, even while worries and fears about other matters seem to be getting in the way. In fact, even the situation of being lost can be a cause for joy, insofar as it helps one to rely on the Lord and to welcome Him to break through the inner storms of the heart. As in other apparently negative situations, the poverty of feeling lost or embarrassed or out of control can move us to trust more deeply in the Lord and to be expectant for His riches of grace, which He will surely bestow in His time and His way. It is a joy to look for these divine benefits even here and now, and to realize that they anticipate the greater riches of eternity.

Joy of surrendering to grace when human efforts fail

One of the first retreats that I gave was offered to a community of sisters out of state. I had been asked to lead the retreat on rather short notice since the other monk who was originally supposed to give the five-day retreat turned out to be unavailable. Still, I did have the time and energy to prepare retreat notes for some ten conferences very carefully. When I gave the conferences, I welcomed the sisters to raise questions or make comments. At one point, I made a remark that was not in my notes. It was to the effect that God's grace is working everywhere, even in the most distressful or unexpected situations. I commented that the phrase "everything is a grace" was somewhere in the New Testament.

Right after I referred to that quote, one sister who was accustomed to ask many questions raised her hand and inquired, "Exactly where in Scripture is that verse?" I said that I was not sure but thought that it was somewhere in Galatians or Romans. "Well, would you please let me know," she replied. (She seemed to be taking assiduous notes and was very insistent about having the correct Scriptural quote.) I told her that I would look up the passage after the conference. I began a search as soon as I had a break from speaking, praying, and eating. I skimmed through all the letters of St. Paul and could not find the verse. I felt very frustrated and did not want to disappoint the sister. On the other hand, I did not want to be obsessed over the issue or to give in to pride in my ability to find the passage. After a while I gave up and decided that I would try again the next day. However, my pride arose again later that evening; so again I searched through the New Testament, and again I could not find the verse. Finally, I realized that I was becoming too preoccupied about the issue; so I left my intensive search to pray Compline and go to bed.

Early the next morning, shortly after I rose, I entered into my daily *lectio divina* by continuing to reflect on the passage where I had left off the previous day. Only a few verses from where I began, I found the verse Romans 4:16 (1970 *New American* version): "All depends on faith. Everything is a grace." What joy I experienced! The very process of my searching and failing proved the truth of the verse. Despite all my frenzied efforts, I had not been able to find what I sought. Then, in an unexpected way and at an unexpected time, the blessing of finding the passage came to me, graciously and freely! In my very next conference I eagerly told the whole story to the sisters, and we all marveled with joy at the amazing way in which grace works—the grace which is everywhere and which is the cause of our joy, even when our frantic human efforts are thwarted.

Joys discovered amid a reluctantly undertaken journey

Not many years ago I received an invitation to attend a religious sister's ceremony for first vows some distance away from the Archabbey. I felt that I could not refuse since I had been friends of her parents for some forty years, and I had become a friend of hers, too. There seemed to be a number of problems with making such a trip. I knew that I could not drive the distance alone. I thought that I could possibly take a plane; but that would be expensive, and I would need people to drive me to airports and to pick me up at airports at either end of the trip. Furthermore, the sister's community could not provide lodging for guests, and I would have to find a place to stay for two nights.

My first thought was to approach another monk who also knew the community of sisters and who might be willing to travel with me. At first he agreed to travel with me; but then, since he was growing increasingly frail because of poor health and age, he told me that he had to withdraw his offer. Then, by chance (and by grace), as I was conversing with a younger monk, I realized that he also was connected with the sisters' community, and he expressed interest in attending the vows ceremony. When I told him the dates, he said that he would be very willing to go with me, provided that I could drive him to an airport on the last day since he was already scheduled to visit his family that day. Well, the problem of traveling <u>to</u> the place had been resolved, but I still needed someone to drive with me on the way home. Again, by chance (and by grace), I was speaking to another young monk who came from the same state as the sisters' community. As it turned out, his family lived not far away from the motherhouse, and he said that he was planning to visit his family not long before my planned trip. Furthermore, he was able to reschedule his departure date so that he could drive back with me. That seemed like wonderful good news; but since he would have a monastery car and since I (and the other monk) would have another monastery car, we still had the problem of getting both cars back to the monastery. It occurred to me (perhaps at the suggestion of another monk) to ask a favor of a particular monk who was known to be generous in driving other monks to their destinations. He was indeed willing, and cheerfully so. The three of us then consulted with one another and came to the decision that the third monk would drive with two of us to a midway point, where the monk already on vacation would meet us in another monastery car. At that point, the "extra monk" would take the other monastery car and drive it back home, while the other two of us would join the other monk (and his mother, who was with him), then drive them to their home with the monastery car that they were using, and finally take that car to our destination. It worked wonderfully, thanks to generosity and mutual consultation, and all of us even were able to eat lunch together at the midway point where we had met. There was genuine joy in the collaboration of brothers to help one another on our journeys and in appreciating the sacrifices that were being made.

Then came the challenges of finding our way in unfamiliar territory. The two of us who originally traveled together were able fairly easily to find the rectory where we had arranged to stay. We were also treated with warm hospitality by the priests who lived there, and that was another cause for joy. The first evening we were scheduled to have dinner at a restaurant with the family and friends of the sister who would be professing vows, and with the help of good directions we found the restaurant without much trouble. However, after dinner it was dark, and finding our way back was not so easy. The restaurant was situated in such a location between two roads that we could not figure out how we had arrived. As a result, we traveled one way and then another, with the hope of seeing a familiar landmark. None showed up. Finally, we saw a sign leading to an interstate highway that could lead us to the center of town where our quarters were; so we took it and then asked for directions from an attendant at a gasoline station to lead us to the rectory.

Early the next morning, before our journey to the 10:00 Mass for the profession, there was a unique opportunity for me to visit a former graduate-school roommate of mine from over 40 years before. The former roommate had told me on the phone that his house would be difficult for me to find on my own; so after my fellow monk and I had eaten an early breakfast, the friend picked me up at the rectory and drove me to his home so that I could spend some time with him, his wife, and his grown son, a student at medical school. Although our visit was brief, it was an occasion of memorable reaquaintance. (I had last visited him and his wife 37 years earlier.) Again, there was joy in seeing an old friend again, along with his family, and in being the recipient of his generous help. Surely, it was a grace-filled opportunity.

Next came the challenge of finding the church where the Mass was to be celebrated. I had good directions from the sister's family, but apparently there was some problem with them since we could not find one of the streets mentioned. Again, a stop at a gasoline station enabled us to make the correct turn and to make our way to the church. The Mass and the vows ceremony were beautiful, moving, and joyful. The two of us had to leave the luncheon-reception a bit early so that I could drive my fellow monk to the airport from which he would fly to visit his mother. Fortunately, the airport was located on the same interstate road on which we had already traveled several times. That was a great blessing!

After I dropped my fellow monk off, another graced-filled event was in store. It turned out that I had two distant cousins who lived in the area. In fact, they lived in an assisted-living home not too far from the interstate, and one of their nieces had given me directions to their residence. Weary from the long day of activity, I made a wrong turn off the interstate and found myself traveling in the wrong direction on the right road. Fortunately, I soon discovered the problem and was able to turn around and make my way to the home where my elderly cousins and a niece of theirs were waiting for me. It was an especially rewarding reunion since one of the two elderly sisters had attended my priestly ordination thirty years earlier, and I had not seen her since. Also, I had never met her sister in person, nor the niece. The four of us had dinner in a special room and enjoyed one another's company as if we had known one another for years. After dinner it was a joy to share family stories and photographs. I was careful to leave early enough so as not to have to drive in the dark, and, with gratitude, I was able to make my way back to the rectory without getting lost. Perhaps also I stayed fairly calm because I was learning that getting lost has its unexpected blessings.

The next morning provided more joys and challenges. The other monk who had been visiting his family and was able to drive back to Latrobe with me had agreed to come to the rectory and church where I was staying so that we could attend the Saturday-morning Mass together and then set out. It was a blessing that the monk's father was free to drive him and his mother to the church and then take the family car home. It was also a grace that the monk's mother had been looking for an opportunity to visit her son at the Archabbey; so she would join us on our journey back. After the Mass the other monk loaded his things into the car that I had been using, and we departed. Being a young monk, he had a G.P.S. that he said would lead us back to the interstate; so we relied on it. However, it apparently had not been updated, as we learned when it twice led us to dead ends. Finally, we decided to ask for directions from a jogger. She told us that we were very near to the interstate and needed only to make two or three turns from our present location. Her directions were very good. Once again, we were in the position of being lost and then found! Despite heavy traffic at certain points, we managed, by grace, to arrive at the Archabbey about 4:25, so that I could hurry to the room where organists practice with cantors before Vespers at 5:00. It happened that I was the only organist available that evening and that the only available cantor was a new junior monk who had never served as cantor before. If I had not arrived on time, he may have had to sing without organ accompaniment, and the very thought of that gave him great anxiety. Thus there was great joy in my timely arrival so that the cantor and I could join the other monks to celebrate Vespers with a sense of good preparation and peace.

In sum, despite all the minor mishaps of that long journey (long for me), there were blessings beyond measure, and even now, seven years later, I must remember them with joy and gratitude.

Seeking joy even amid a life-threatening danger

One Sunday in February not many years ago, I needed to drive back to the Archabbey from an overnight stay in a parish about 75 minutes east of the Archabbey. The weather had been clear at the time of my arrival at the parish on Saturday, but then early on Sunday morning a heavy snowfall began. During my second Sunday Mass I could not help feeling anxious about the forthcoming drive home. A number of generous parishioners offered to drive me back to the Archabbey despite the danger and the extra three hours it would take for the round trip. I was tempted to accept the offer but in the end asked those parishioners simply to pray for me. Of course, they promised to do so.

After a stretch of fairly level road, I turned onto a highway with a succession of fairly steep hills and low valleys. On one of the first hills my car skidded, and in my panic I did all that I could to go off to the side of the road. I was grateful that there was a fairly level grassy, if snow-covered, area where I could just stay and rest until I could regain some courage. I had never been in such a frightening situation before. What if no one came to help me? What if the snow continued? What if I were to freeze to death? In any case, all I could do was to turn on flashing lights and implore the Lord in prayer (perhaps I did some *lectio divina* or prayed Midday Prayer; I was so nervous that I could hardly think), that He would do something to free me from the critical situation. It was some fifteen or twenty minutes after my going off the road that a welcome vehicle approached my car. Coming out of the truck was a young man, who asked if he could assist me. Amazingly, he was on his way to a social event in that snowy weather. It did not take me long to explain that I was stuck and needed help to get back on the road to Latrobe. There seemed to be no way in which I could negotiate the car up the rest of the hill or the several hills that would follow. However, the man, named Jimmy, had a chain in his truck (that seemed to be a little miracle!), and he worked hard to attach the chain to the bottom of my car. Then he pulled me up a short distance and helped me back into a driveway. While he was exerting all this effort, a plow came by on the other side of the road. The young man suggested that I wait in the driveway until the plow would come to clear our side of the road, as he said it surely would. Beyond that, he asked if I needed to contact anyone. When I said that I had no way of doing so, he offered me the use of his cell phone, and with appropriate instructions from him, I phoned the prior of our community to inform him that I was stuck in a snowstorm and would arrive home late. Then the kind young man went on his way, and despite my extreme anxiety over my predicament, I could not help but feel much gratitude for his generosity and the joy that went along with that gratitude. Truly I had been visited by an "angel in disguise"!

Some fifteen minutes after Jimmy left me, the plow did, in fact, come by on my side of the road, and I was relatively content to follow a row of five or six cars behind the plow for several miles. Then, alas, the plow turned off to the right, but the road ahead was still fairly clear so that I had enough courage to proceed. Somehow, only with God's grace, I managed to drive rather slowly and cautiously to Latrobe, where, fortunately, the streets were merely wet. Having been practically glued to the steering wheel for a number of miles, I arrived in our parking lot with my hands probably stiffer than they had ever been before; but I was at home, safe and sound! On arriving, I hurried to return the keys to the prior's office. There I found the prior and told my story to him, and he listened compassionately. We also agreed that if any similar situation should develop in the future, then my best approach would be to call him when I saw a storm coming on a Sunday and seek to stay overnight one more day, in the hope that roads would be clear the next day.

Of course, there had been little or no tangible joy during the ordeal of being trapped in a snowstorm. However, there were graces even during the crisis that were the cause of a subtle joy. When I first went off the road, I had the grace to pray, no matter how unfocused and anxious my prayer seemed to be. (I had the Midday Prayer from St. Vincent in the front passenger's seat.) Also, I had the gift of trusting, amid my deep fears, that the Lord would somehow come to my aid. He had rescued me hundreds of times in the past from other dangers, less critical though they may have been. When Jimmy approached with his truck, I felt inexpressible gratitude and joy, as I also did when the plow came by my side of the road. In retrospect, most certainly, I can rejoice in the grace to keep praying amid terrible distress, in the great kindness of a total stranger, in the hope given to me by the driver of the snow plow (unknown to me though he was), and in the courage God gave me to keep driving safely until I reached home despite my extraordinary anxiety. There had been graces, too, in the parishioners' offer to drive me home and in their considerate efforts to brush the snow off my car before I had set out. The mere memory of the whole incident causes me joy and gratitude for what the Lord has done. Because of the event, I am determined to remember the powerful message from Romans 4:16: "All depends on faith. Everything is a grace!" One lesson from the instructive incident is that fearful, frenzied efforts, driven by mere human determination, lead to anxiety and fear, whereas prayerful human striving that cooperates with grace results in peace and ultimate joy.

Discovery of Joy in Growing Old

However much we sometimes would like to deny it, we are all growing older and headed for death—and, with the certainty of faith, eternal life. Most of us, by the time we are in our 50's, 60's, or 70's, though we may not consider ourselves "old," have experienced some diminishments of body and perhaps also of mind. As I write these reflections, I realize that this year has been a time of unusually numerous medical procedures for me. In the spring I underwent a second root canal (the first took place last year), and now I await a tooth extraction and two cataract surgeries. I also underwent some sessions of physical therapy (the first in my life) for chronic neck pain. Furthermore, I find myself taking a number of medications or applying various creams for conditions from head to foot, and the number of these physical remedies is not likely to decrease. Where is the blessing, and where is the joy in all of this?

First, the physical diminishments remind me of the approach of death, even if it may be some years away. My body is slowly crumbling. I was reminded of this when my dentist said of a badly cracked tooth, "There's nothing more I can do for it." Someday a doctor may say the same of my whole body! That should be good news. I can find joy in the reality of facing death because for us Christians it means a closer relationship with Christ, and He is our joy..

Secondly, the medications and procedures remind me of my

dependence on others in various ways. Of course, we are always dependent on others, even in the vigor of adolescence and early adulthood, though we may treasure an illusory independence. At this point in life (partly because I belong to a monastic community), I depend on others to drive me to certain procedures, to supply me with medications, to pay medical bills, and to perform procedures that keep my health from declining too quickly. This dependence, while I must not take advantage of it, is a reminder of the "communion of saints." In the love of Christ, we do and should depend on other brothers and sisters in Christ for all sorts of spiritual, emotional, and physical benefits. It can and should be a joy to call to mind such a truth. We are not alone, though we sometimes feel lonely. Not only do we receive immense graces directly from God, but we also have the wonderful support, by His own loving plan, of saints and angels and of the prayers and works of mercy of many, many people on earth. Of course, I am called to do my part to help others who depend on me. In all of this exchange of benefits in love, we all together grow closer to Christ as members of His Body. That growth is truly a cause of joy!

Our ultimate dependence on God is also a reminder that He, and ultimately He alone, is the giver of all gifts. He gave us our bodies; He directly created our souls; He sanctified us in baptism; He graciously comes to us in the sacraments; and He will take us to Himself when we die, whether we go directly to heaven or need to undergo some spiritual therapy in purgatory. To know that we are falling into the hands of a loving God and, even in weakness, able to expand our hearts in loving communion with the Blessed Trinity is indeed another good reason for rejoicing even as we experience the gradual decline of our bodies. Indeed, on the Last Day, He will give us glorified bodies that will endure eternally in communion with Him and with all the saints and angels. This future condition will be one of supreme joy!

CHAPTER 10

Freedom from the Need to Look Happy or Feel Cheerful

As these reflections come to a close, it might be helpful to stress once more the difference between the Christian joy that causes one to "rejoice always" and fleeting, observable happiness. In dealing with the call for Christians to be joyful, even at all times, emphasis is sometimes given on the importance of *looking* joyful or having happy *feelings*. Some people, whether Christian or not, are gifted with naturally cheerful dispositions and the ability to come across to others as cheerful. Such gifts can be used to glorify God and give strong witness to others. However, not everyone possesses such gifts. Perhaps it would be ideal if every Christian could look and feel joyful at every moment, but such is not the case. In fact, to insist that Christians offer a happy appearance could have the opposite effect; a Christian who tries to look cheerful even though such outward joy is not natural to him could end up feeling dejected and guilty for not being able to fulfill an unrealizable ideal. The joy of Easter faith cannot demand that Christians look or feel joyful, although at times a Christian may, out of charity, need to put on a smile or ask the Lord to lift up his dejected feelings in order for him to "get out of himself," to live in deeper faith, or to give assurances of faith to others.

In his book *Nomad of the Spirit*, German Trappist abbot Fr. Bernardin Schellenberger warns against the notion that the Christian must always look happy or the illusion that joining a religious community is like entering into a paradise of deep, uplifting prayer and spiritually energizing relationships. He points out that the deprivations of religious life and the restrictions demanded by the vows can open us more fully to the evil within us as well as to the misery of the world. Sometimes vocational materials show young, smiling religious romping in a seemingly peaceful, care-free environment. Most vowed religious probably experience this brighter side of life occasionally, but it is hardly the whole picture. Like lay Christians, they should not feel compelled to put on happy faces. Leaving behind some pleasures of life in the "world" for a life of self-denial and disciplined prayer can assist a person to acknowledge multiple disorders in his or her heart and the need to break down many interior barriers between God and the individual if one is to make progress in holiness. This process can be very painful and make it impossible to keep a cheerful disposition. Fr. Bernardin comments, "Joy, enthusiasm, experience of redemption - these are expected of Christians today if they are to have credibility. And they expect it of themselves. ... But is it really so certain that every Christian committed to a life of faith can, indeed must, radiate joy? Is not *the* symbol of Christianity now and always the cross, the image of the Redeemer nailed to the cross, and not a serenely smiling Buddha? And what about Mary, the most shining model for believers, ... the Mother of Sorrows? There is the sadness of the tired, lukewarm, half-hearted Christians who do not live in the freedom of the sons of God, but as morose servants more or less resigned to God's will. This sadness is truly bad. It is caused by lack of faith, lack of consistency, lack of depth. ...Now, however, I wish to speak about a different kind of Christian sadness: the sorrow of the person who takes the risk of faith; the pain and suffering of the person who has set out upon the Imitation of Christ. ... [T]he thesis that living faith and visible joy belong together does not hold in the naïve sense in which it is often presented" (*NS*, pp. 74-75). Fr. Bernardin then goes on to explain that external cheerfulness is not always possible or healthy. True, deep, interior joy, that is, the fruit of the Holy Spirit, is not at all opposed to a profound experience of sorrow as a share in the Cross.

Furthermore, Fr. Bernardin actually writes about the value of a sorrowful disposition in Christian life. He states, "Joy that is visible to all, contagious for all, is a charisma, a gracious gift from God. There are people who receive it. But Jesus also has disciples who now mourn and weep, and he calls them blessed because some day they shall laugh (Matt. 5:4; par. Luke 6:21). The ancients knew of the 'gift of tears,' of the 'contrition of the heart.' Benedict wants his monks always to go about 'with lowered heads' and to 'avoid laughter.' One should not misinterpret this as a duty to be sorrowful and to vegetate. On the contrary, it can express a call to *com-miserate*, to suffer along with the wretchedness and imperfection of the world" (*NS*, p. 78).

Relevant to this healthy sort of sorrow are Fr. Michael Casey's comments on the sixth, seventh, and eighth degrees of humility in his book *A Guide to Living in the Truth: Saint Benedict's Teaching on Humility*. He covers these three steps in the chapter "Yielding to Others." Fr. Michael writes, "From the point of view of the individual these are difficult steps to understand. From a more social angle they are a little more acceptable. Nobody contributes less to the common life than those who constantly make demands or attribute absolute importance to their individual desires over the needs of the community as a whole. ... Yielding to others is a concrete means of demonstrating respect and love. It is not abject submission, but it derives from a strong and fervent spirit" (*GLT*, p. 141). Reflecting on being a "bad and worthless worker," Fr. Michael says that the essence of this step is the call for contentment even amid lowliness and trials. He asserts, "Everyone passes through times of adversity: the sign of one whose heart is becoming uniquely fixed on God is that these external fluctuations have less power to affect moods. Patience has helped to cultivate a quiet mind, and self-disclosure has made one less inclined to subterfuge. ...My identity and status are not dependent on the good will of the abbot. They derive from being created unique by God my Father, redeemed by Jesus Christ my brother, and uniquely gifted by the Holy Spirit. I belong to the communion of saints, all of whom recognize me as one of themselves. I don't need a stripe on the sleeve to convince me that I have worth. The approval and affirmation of others and the opportunities these present are important to me, but if I lose them I am not automatically bereft of standing in the eyes of God" (*GLT*, pp. 143-144). Regarding St. Benedict's use of the terms "inferior to all" and "a worm, not a human being," Fr. Michael writes, "A genuine attraction to be filled with the lowliness of Christ leads us to take steps to ensure that the press releases we issue about ourselves are truthful not only in fact but in implication. This means that they are made in the mindfulness of our own limitations and of the ugly scar tissue that remains. ... What Benedict intends by this step is to draw our attention to the importance of inner conviction. Humble attitudes must derive from a deep experience of our own indigence. It is this realization that grounds our capacity to welcome the salvation Christ offers us. ... To be humble before God is to acknowledge that all is gift except what I have spoiled" (*GLT*, pp. 149-150). This heartfelt acknowledgment that all is gift is a major source of true joy.

Perhaps the least palatable verses of the *Rule* are those of the sixth, seventh, and eighth steps of humility. As Fr. Michael Casey explains, living these steps, contrary to first impressions, does not take away from our dignity but rather enhances out true dignity in God's eyes. Finding contentment in the meanest of things, knowing oneself to be "inferior," and sticking to the "common rule" are surely not formulas for a cheerful appearance or glad feelings. However, St. Benedict is telling us that, like the practices that open us to joy during Lent, the recommendations in these steps of humility nurture a deep, interior, and lasting joy that results from a growing communion with God. These negative-sounding steps of humility are very much in harmony with our Easter faith, which proclaims that we have been redeemed through the Passion, Death, and Resurrection of Christ, that Christ has raised us up with Him (cf. Col 3:1), and that in baptism we have received a share in the divine nature of God Himself. Therefore, such precepts and practices are very much in harmony with a joyful Christian life.

At this point it might also be beneficial to recognize that there are different levels of joy on the spiritual journey. Normally, when a person is converted from a life of sin, unbelief, or lukewarmness to a life of zealous faith, he or she experiences much manifest joy in almost everything - or so it seems. Then, however, if the person is open to God's graces, there are successive "dark nights" that purify the soul from its attachments. The joy of material pleasures, emotional pleasures, and even "spiritual" pleasures must give way to joy in God alone. Author Fr. Marc Foley, O.C.D., describes this progression skillfully in his book *The Ascent of Mount Carmel: Reflections,* which assists the reader to understand St. John of the Cross's notions of spiritual growth. Fr. Foley says of an early transition, "The soul is filled with joy, for the whole world seems to sparkle. The joy of doing God's will and loving one's neighbor is the bright atmosphere in which it lives and breathes. But one day the sun is shrouded and the whole world turns gray" (*AMC*, p. 10). The honeymoon is over! Over periods of time and after successive purifications, the soul ideally learns to delight in God alone. The soul needs "dark nights" if it is to go beyond comparatively superficial joys to this highest joy. Fr. Foley reflects, "John [St. John of the Cross] seems to be saying that souls who seek their happiness [joy] in God alone will find delight in *all things* because they will be content with what God provides" (*AMC*, p. 25). Toward the end of his book, Fr. Foley includes the chapters "Joy in Temporal Goods," "Joy in Natural Goods," "Joy in Sensory Goods," "Joy in Moral Goods," "Joy in Supernatural Goods," and "Joy in Spiritual Goods." Each of these joys can be good and holy, but they can also be the cause of unhealthy attachments. God lovingly leads the faithful Christian away from each type of joy to higher joys and ultimately to rejoicing in Him alone. For example, Fr. Foley points out, "...supernatural goods should be rejoiced in to the extent that God is loved and served through them Those possessing a supernatural gift are vulnerable to pride. They can be tempted to use their gift for the sake of self-aggrandizement" (*AMC*, p. 196). To conclude his book, Fr. Foley writes, "[A]ll things are good and are meant to be means that will lead us to God. However, they can be obstacles if we choose to take up a possessive relationship to them. John [St. John of the Cross] puts before us both the misery that comes from a possessive heart and the joy that God grants to a soul that loves freely" (*AMC*, p. 217). Let us, then, seek this ultimate joy of living totally for God!

Reaching this joy, as Fr. Michael Casey so clearly states, requires us to embrace humility and the fundamental truth that God is everything and that I am nothing. Often it takes experiences of humiliation to come to know God's unmerited love for us and the great dignity He has given us in Christ as a completely free gift. Too frequently we base our sense of worth on our success, our good feelings, our wealth, our intelligence, our appearance, our ability to influence others, or some other human criterion. During one Paschal Triduum I was sent to a parish an hour and a half away from the monastery for the Mass of the Lord's Supper and the Commemoration of Our Lord's Passion and Death. During my journey I was surprised by snow squalls and heavy winds that I feared would blow the car off the road or into other vehicles; the dangers reminded me that only by God's grace did I arrive at the parish safe and sound. (I was much tempted to neglect gratitude and to protest that there should not be such wintry weather on April 1!) It was a grace, too, that on my arrival I encountered the main master of ceremonies, who shortly thereafter went through the procedures for the evening Mass with me. I needed to be oriented as to how that particular parish celebrated the Holy Thursday Mass; besides, I had not presided at such a Mass for some 34 years. Despite all the help, I ended up preaching my homily for Good Friday on Holy Thursday. Fortunately, the next morning I had ample time to write a new homily for Good Friday. Unfortunately, I felt rather sick since I had eaten something that upset me. By the afternoon I was well enough to preside at the Stations of the Cross at noon and the Commemoration at 1:00. Then, at my departure, I somehow got lost in that small town. After some distressful meandering, I saw a sign to the next town that oriented me; there was another unmerited gift. In sum, the two days provided me with an adventure of many ups and downs, with evidence of my folly and, even more, of God's grace. I could say with St. Paul, "Everything is grace!" (Rom 4:16). Amid all the trials that left me weary and without outward cheerfulness, I was once more, through humiliations, learning the formula for true joy.

My experience of the Easter Vigil, here at the Archabbey, was very different but also grace-filled in a hidden way. I typically cannot stay awake during the Vigil, especially during the long Scriptural readings proclaimed in darkness, and this past year was no exception. In fact, I seemed to feel more miserable than usual during the most festive of all Masses. How I wish to experience the joy of the Resurrection and have a lively participation in the liturgy, but I fall terribly short! I could not even remember anything from the homily, which, I'm sure, was a very fine one. Amid the celebration of new life in Christ, I felt like a lifeless rag. Of course, the problem was with <u>me</u>, and not with the liturgy. Perhaps, however, there is a powerful lesson here as well. We finite humans have very little control over our physical and emotional dispositions. Even when we "do our best" (and it is hard to tell what really is our best), our dispositions can be totally contrary to what we would wish them to be. In such situations we sense that we are "worthless workmen," people who see ourselves as "inferior to all," like worms and not human beings. Along with our misery, compounded with disappointment in ourselves, we must know in faith that Christ comes to redeem us by entering into our distress. Despite our unworthiness and confusion, He graciously grants us new and divine life!

Thus, as with the Sacred Scriptures themselves, not all parts of the *Holy Rule* are naturally appealing; but with the help of prayerful reflection and of consultation with reliable commentaries, we can begin to "see the light" - and even the opportunity for joy - in unappealing phrases. It can be a struggle to find meaning in certain passages, but we must trust that God has given these to us for some reason. In fact, whatever meaning we come to find in them should result in drawing us closer to Christ and thus to a deep, joyful communion with the Blessed Trinity. As many commentators tell us, the whole *Rule* is Christ-centered and is meant to lead us more readily to Christ on our journeys of faith. For example, to consider oneself "a poor and worthless workman" seems to be in harmony with Our Lord's saying that a servant should eat and drink only when his master is finished. Should the master be "grateful to that servant because he did what was commanded? So should it be with you. When you have done all you have been commanded, say, 'We are unprofitable servants; we have done what we were obliged to do'" (Lk 17:9-10). Our Lord, who is surely a model for St. Benedict, often teaches us humility. Sometimes His statements seem harsh or even impossible to live out; but if we ponder them perseveringly, we can begin to understand the mysterious truths underlying the strange words and see the value of incorporating these truths into our lives. We can recognize how unlike Christ we are when we, outwardly or secretly, try to take credit for our work or even compare our work with others' work in order to come out looking better. We can see how much we need to know ourselves as nothing and useless without God's grace, which alone makes everything beautiful, valuable, and useful. Likewise, the passage of being "truly a worm, not a man" is taken from Psalm 22, which Our Lord prayed from the Cross. He Himself, though He was God, was humbled in the most abject way; and yet it was this miserable humiliation that brought us salvation. Who, then, are we to protest against being convinced that we are "inferior to all and of less value" (*RB* 7:52) when such a disposition brings us closer to Our Lord? Thus all admonitions about humility provide opportunities to unite ourselves with Christ, especially in His Passion. Again, this process of Christ's uniting us with Himself, often through trials, is a cause for joy.

Furthermore, such words remind us of the truth that we can do nothing good without grace. When we are allowed by God to feel our utter misery, we have an occasion to remind ourselves of this total dependence on grace and the ready availability of grace. Too often we seek to evaluate ourselves by other standards, all of which are enslaving. God cares only how faithful we are in responding to His grace, which is His own life reaching us through His freely given gifts. It is liberating to know that we need not feel or appear bright and cheerful on Easter Sunday (or at the Easter Vigil) or, on the other hand, feel or appear sorrowful on Good Friday. Feelings come and go; only God's promises and the assurance of His grace (to which we can close ourselves when we are depending on feelings or appearances or achievements) are unshakable.

At all times and seasons, it is important to remember that our only ultimate fulfillment and our only complete joy is heavenly communion with Christ and all the saints and angels. Our life on earth and our struggle to live in Christian faith are meant to be an arduous battle against sinful inclinations and outer evils. We are not promised a bed of roses. However, we need not and should not be stuck in gloom. To cling to feelings of being worthless and sub-human can be an excuse for sloth. Amid our dispositions of darkness and gloom, we are obliged to focus on Christ and not on ourselves; we are challenged not to give in to grouchiness or grumbling, as St. Benedict so often remind us. We do not have to put on an air of cheerfulness, but neither must we wallow in misery or seek pity from others. All of that goes against charity and faith. One of my favorite Easter hymns, "Now the Green Blade Rises," includes the verse, "When our hearts are wintry, grieving, or in pain, Your touch can call us back to life again, Fields of our hearts that dead and bare have been: Love is come again like wheat arising green." Christ the Lord is ever present to redeem us here and now and to lead us to heavenly glory; so we need always to rejoice, even if our joy is subdued and hidden behind a naturally saddened façade.

Praying the psalms, whether in the Liturgy of the Hours or in our personal *lectio divina*, can be a grace-filled antidote to being stuck in ourselves, in our feelings, in our ambitions, or in our prideful imaginings, all of which lead to unhealthy sorrow and detract from joy. One speaker at a presentation to Oblates in Latrobe, an expert in the psalms, reminded the audience that there is a psalm for every human emotion and situation. Whatever may be our disposition, we can find verses in one psalm or another with which we can identify. Praying psalms that match our dispositions can bring perspective to our situations, can unite us with others who share our condition, and can help us to focus on Christ, who surely prayed all the psalms and shared in their expressions of relationship with God the Father. On the other hand, praying only the psalms that match our given dispositions could be spiritually unhealthy. We need to pray those psalms that "go against our grain" in order to unite ourselves with those who feel differently. When we are feeling worthless, like a worm and no man, we should still pray psalms of thanksgiving and praise because others are thankful and praise-filled, and surely Our Lord wants us to know the glory that is in store for us. When we are feeling glorious, then we should still pray the psalms of lament, even the darkest of verses, since others in the Church are undergoing such darkness and we may yet need to undergo desolations in order to be purified of prideful tendencies. Praying whatever psalms are provided in the Divine Office can be a powerful remedy for living in a self-centered world since we are assimilating the inspired words that God, through the Church, is giving us and not limiting ourselves to the passages that offer affirmation or comfort.

In sum, Christ, who surely was not always radiant with joy, calls us to conformity with Himself and to a joy that results from likeness to Him. Through the difficult steps of humility and the challenging words of Scripture, Christ summons us to leave behind our prideful tendencies and to live in total reliance on God's grace, which is the source of our true joy. It is He alone who can order our lives in a way that leads to perfect fulfillment in union with Him. Thus we must ever make "the love of Christ … come before all else" (RB 4:21) and "prefer nothing whatever to Christ" (72:11). In Him alone do we find our joy, our hope, and the way to our "heavenly home" (73:8).

CHAPTER 11

Conclusion:
Jesus Christ as the Source
of All Our Genuine Joy

Here it is, November of 2020, and I am still working ploddingly on this project on Christian, Benedictine joy. Perhaps I should rejoice that this project has not been under my control. In fact, I have found almost no time to work on it except during my annual summer vacations from 1994 to 1997 and then during the coronavirus pandemic in the spring of this year and then, less intensively, in subsequent months. My inability to control the progress of this collection of reflections may be a sign that God's grace is nudging me not to rush or plan too much or to set any firm deadlines. If it is indeed God's grace that has governed the pace of this project, then I must rejoice in this slowness.

Before the revision of the *Roman Missal* in 2011, I discovered "joy" in the opening oration for the Twenty-First Sunday in Ordinary Time. It read as follows: "Father, help us to seek the values that will bring us lasting joy in this changing world. In our desire for what you promise make us one in mind and heart." (The equivalent prayer in the current missal reads, "O God, who cause the minds of the faithful to unite in a single purpose, grant your people to love what you command and to desire what you promise, that, amid the uncertainties of this world, our hearts may be fixed on that place where true gladness is found.") Whether one uses the terms "joy" or "gladness," these words ask for the grace to set our desires on the eternal values proclaimed by Christ, the values which have already given us a taste of lasting joy, the only values that can unite diverse people in their common search for God. We know that our desires are frustrated by <u>not</u> being set on what God promises; and so, as perhaps as they should be, our hearts remain restless and dissatisfied. The alternative prayer in the pre-2011 *Sacramentary* included the request, "Give your people the joy of hearing your word in every sound and of longing for your presence more than for life itself." On this earth joy comes in loving obedience to God's loving commands, even while we know that we are often deaf and disobedient out of confusion or stubbornness. On this earth true joy accompanies our unfulfilled longings only when we realize that they are meant to be directed to embracing God's gracious plan of redemption in Jesus Christ. How amazing that we would even dare to seek false earthly joys! Should we not prefer death to losing a sense of God's saving presence? Only with grace could we utter a prayer of longing for God's presence more than for earthly life and well-being. Only with grace could we let this divine joy override our ephemeral attractions. Only with grace can we sift and sort among many desires, some of them so perverted yet so tempting, to discover the true and lasting joy that will endure when we are fully surrendered and raised up. Indeed, may all the attractions of this changing world serve only to bring us the peace and joy of God's Kingdom, which this world cannot give.

In my *lectio divina* on the Book of the Prophet Baruch, I have also found references to the joy to which St. Benedict invites us. The book addresses the Jewish people in the misery of exile in Babylon, with the loss of their country, their temple in Jerusalem, and their sacred customs. Nonetheless, God promises them, after a period of purification, a future of joyful return to the Promised Land, and that hope of return gives them reason to rejoice even in the midst of exile. In Chapter 3, Baruch reminds the people that even nature rejoices at being in the presence of God. He asserts of the stars, "Before whom [God] the stars at their posts shine and rejoice; when He calls them, they answer, 'Here we are!', shining with joy for their Maker" (Bar 3: 34-35). Later in Chapter 4, the city of Jerusalem speaks as a mother to her children in exile: "I have trusted in the Eternal God for your welfare, and joy has come to me from the Holy One because of the mercy that will reach you from your eternal savior. With mourning and lament I sent you forth, but God will give you back to me with enduring gladness and joy" (Bar 4: 22-23). A few verses later, this joyful good news is reinforced: "As your hearts have been disposed to stray from God, turn now ten times the more to seek him; for he who has brought disaster upon you will, in saving you, bring you back this enduring joy" (Bar 4: 28-29).

Just as the Israelites were purified of their waywardness during their exile in Babylon, so are we intent on graces of repentance and conversion during our pilgrimages of Lent and the ongoing pilgrimage of Christian life. Just as the Israelites experienced joyful anticipation of return to the Holy Land even while they endured the grief of exile, so can we experience joy during this life because of the graces that God is giving us to be purified of our sinful ways so that we can celebrate a more complete return to God when our eternal Easter arrives. The joy of Lent is an anticipation of the joy of Easter, and yet we know that our celebration of Easter on this earth is still marred by recurring imperfections so that even this joy is fleeting and not full. Easter joy only anticipates the fullness of joy that we believe we shall experience in heaven, the joy that emerges from our being raised up with Christ eternally. Let us, then, strive to welcome the Holy Spirit's fruit of joy during Lent and during every day of our Christian journeys, for that openness to joy provides good practice for the bliss of our eternal place in heaven with all the angels and saints and with the very Blessed Trinity, the source of all true joy.

A hymn that our monastic community uses for some solemnities and feasts of the Lord beautifully expresses the joy that we can have on earth and the fullness of joy that we hope to have in heaven. The third, fourth, and fifth verses of the hymn "The Head That Once Was Crowned with Thorns" read as follows:

> The joy of all who dwell above,
> The joy of all below,
> To whom he manifests his love,
> And grants his name to know.
>
> To them the cross with all its shame,
> With all its grace, is given;
> Their name an everlasting name;
> Their joy the joy of heaven.
>
> They suffer with their Lord below;
> They reign with him above;
> Their profit and their joy to know
> The mystery of his love.

Thomas Kelly, 1789-1854.

These words confirm the truth that Christ is our true and only lasting joy, both on earth and in heaven. Because of His love, because of our share in His love, and even because of our share in His cross, we can have an abundance of joy on this earth as we eagerly anticipate the fullness of joy in heaven, where we hope to reign with Christ, in His love, forever. Indeed, in Jesus Christ, in Him and Him alone do our hearts find authentic joy. Let us strive to do what we can to know this joy ever more fully and be ready to proclaim this joy to others so that all may come to know Christ and the wonderful mystery of His love. May this book provide one small contribution to the proclamation of Gospel joy. Extending this joy to others gives us a share in the disposition of St. John the Evangelist when he asserted, "We are writing this so that our joy may be complete" (1 Jn 1:4).

AFTERWORD

Many years ago, I came across a most intriguing story told by Father Edward Hays. It concerned a successful man who had become restless in his pursuits. More than anything else in life he desired to know the Truth. Therefore, he left in search of it. He wandered the earth for years, visiting gurus and grey-bearded scholars. He climbed holy mountains, visited temples, and questioned mystics. But he did not find the Truth.

After many long years he received a clue that on a certain hilltop, in a distant land, he would finally find the Truth. With great eagerness, he traveled to that far land and climbed the difficult mountain. At the very top, he came to a dark cave. There, sitting at its entrance, was the most distasteful and repulsive creature he had ever laid eyes upon.

The seeker spoke, "I am here after a long and difficult journey that has taken years. I have come seeking the Truth!" Motioning him in, the creature led him back into the damp darkness of the mountain. In the blackness of the cave, the creature spoke, and the voice was the most beautiful voice he had ever heard. He KNEW then that he had indeed found Truth!

They spent a year together in the cave, and he learned the Truth. When their time together was ending and the man was preparing to return to his family and the world, he asked his teacher, "What can I do to thank you for this most precious treasure you have given me?" The creature leaned close and whispered hesitantly in his ear, "When you tell others of your experience and people ask about me, tell them … tell them … that I was beautiful!"

Father Hays did not provide a moral of the story, but I will.

Some, skeptics and cynics, might say there is no such thing as

123

Truth—even Truth is dishonest! I prefer the explanation that Truth, like beauty and meaning, often lies beneath the surface. And anyone who espouses the Truth is truly beautiful!

Readers might be excused if they approach this book with some skepticism: "joy in Lent" sounds like a contradiction, an oxymoron. "Joy amid suffering" hardly seems like a truism. Yet, Father Donald has done a masterful job of revealing joy where it is not ordinarily thought present and discovering joy where it is commonly presumed absent.

Joy is accurately defined as possessing God or at least being in the process of acquiring Him. This is in distinction from seeing joy as the happiness that emanates from the physical or emotional pleasure of having what we desire at a particular point in time. So, contrary to popular thought, joy can be present regardless of whether one feels happy, sad, or neither.

The notion of joy in Lent as mentioned by Saint Benedict in his Rule also benefits from Father Donald's exposition on the topic. Lent, with its deprivations and penitential practices, conjures up nearly the direct opposite of joy. But when seen as tools for disciplining ourselves as part of our ongoing conversion to Christ, Lenten activities are indeed joyful!

Joy is not usually immediately associated with the Bible, Old or New Testaments. Again, however, Father Donald presents a wonderful summary of the Old Testament as filled with rejoicing at the faithfulness of God's people. Moreover, the Resurrection of Christ from the dead, the focus of the New Testament, is surely cause for rejoicing as a result of our ultimate share in that final victory over sin and death. Saint Paul, in particular, finds joy in the spirit by participation in Christ's own sacrifice of self-giving love. In tribulations we find the Church progressing in ushering in Christ's rule over the world, truly a cause for rejoicing despite apparent anxiety and grief.

Similarly, Father Donald unveils the presence of joy and causes for rejoicing in the Lenten and Easter liturgies of the Church, recent papal documents, and classic and contemporary authors of literature on spirituality. Most revelatory is his treatment of finding joy in everyday life, even in outward distress. He does the reader a great service by locating essential joy in the most unexpected places: in sacrifice, uncertainty, difficult personalities, thwarted benign efforts, failure, illness, danger, aging, and death. When these situations confront us, as they surely will do, a discerning spirit can uncover joy.

In this book, Father Donald has taught the Truth: that joy is often considerably more than first impressions and frequently lies below the surface. Joy is rooted in the source of all goodness and Truth here and hereafter—Jesus Christ the Lord, Who is omnipresent! Therefore, when we speak of all human experience, we can indeed say, "There is joy."

Archabbot Martin de Porres Bartel, O.S.B.
Saint Vincent Archabbey

REFERENCES
AND ABBREVIATIONS

(JL) Belsole, Fr. Kurt, O.S.B., *Joy in Lent: Gaudium in Chapter 49 of the Regula Benedicti: The Monastic and Liturgical Contexts* (Ph.D. Dissertation, Pontificum Athenaeum S. Anselmo de Urbe, 1993)

(JiL) Belsole, Fr. Kurt, O.S.B., same as *JL* but only excerpts from the dissertation (Latrobe, PA: Saint Vincent Archabbey, 1995)

(BPO) Benedict XVI, Pope (at the time Joseph Cardinal Ratzinger), *Behold the Pierced One: An Approach to Christian Christology* (San Francisco: Ignatius Press, 1986)

(IC), Benedict XVI, Pope (at the time of the first edition Joseph Cardinal Ratzinger), *Introduction to Christianity* (San Francisco: Ignatius Press, 1990, 2004)

(MYJ) Benedict XVI, Pope (at the time Joseph Cardinal Ratzinger), *Ministers of Your Joy: Reflections on Priestly Spirituality* (London: St. Pauls Publishing, 1989)

(VD) Benedict XVI, Pope, *The Word of the Lord* (post-synodal apostolic exhortation *Verbum Domini*, September 30, 2010) (Boston: Pauline Books & Media, 2010)

(AL) Burrows, Sr. Ruth, *Ascent to Love: The Spiritual Teaching of St. John of the Cross* (Denville, NJ: Dimension Books, 1987)

(SISPT) Cantalamessa, Fr. Raniero, O.F.M.Cap., *Sober Intoxication of the Spirit, Part Two: Born Again of Water and the Spirit* (tr. by Marsha Daigle-Williamson, Ph.D.) (Cincinnati, OH: Servant Books, 2012)

(GLT) Casey, Fr. Michael, O.C.S.O., A *Guide to Living in the Truth: Saint Benedict's Teaching on Humility* (Liguori, MO: Liguori/ Triumph, 2001)

(IS) Chautard, Dom Jean-Baptiste, *Inner Strength for Active Apostles: How to Win Souls without Losing Your Own* (Manchester, NH: Sophia Institute Press, 2003)

(AMC) Foley, Fr. Marc, O.C.D., *The Ascent of Mount Carmel: Reflections* (Washington, DC: ICS Publications, 2013)

(EG) Francis, Pope, *Evangelii Gaudium (The Joy of the Gospel*, apostolic exhortation, November 24, 2013) (Erlanger, KY: The Dynamic Catholic Institute, 2014)

(WG) Heufelder, Abbot Emmanuel, O.S.B., *The Way to God According to the Rule of St. Benedict*, tr. by Luke Eberle, O.S.B. (Kalamazoo, MI: Cistercian Publications, 1983)

(DM) John Paul II, Pope Saint, *Dives in Misericordia* (encyclical, *Rich in Mercy*, November 30, 1980) (Washington, DC: United States Catholic Conference, 1981)

(EE) John Paul II, Pope Saint, *Ecclesia de Eucharistia*, (encyclical, "On the Eucharist in Its Relationship to the Church," April 17, 2003) (Washington, DC: United States Catholic Conference, 2003)

(EV) John Paul II, Pope Saint, *Evangelium Vitae* (encyclical, "The Gospel of Life: On the Value and Inviolability of Human Life," March

25, 1995) (Washington, DC: United States Catholic Conference, 1995)

(TMA) John Paul II, Pope Saint, *Tertio Millennio Adveniente* (apostolic letter, "On Preparation for the Jubilee of the Year 2000," November 10, 1994) (Boston: Pauline Books and Media, 1994)

(CB) Kolodiejchuk, Fr. Brian, M.C. (editor, with his commentary), *Mother Teresa: Come Be My Light: The Private Writings of the 'Saint of Calcutta'* (New York: Doubleday, 2007)

(SC) Mele, Fr. Joseph, *The Sacred Conversation: The Art of Catholic Preaching and the New Evangelization* (Steubenville, OH: Emmaus Road Publishing, 2013)

(ND) Nault, Fr. Jean-Charles, O.S.B., *The Noonday Devil: Acedia, the Unnamed Evil of Our Times,* tr. by Michael J. Miller (San Francisco: Ignatius Press, 2013)

(OCJ) Paul VI, Pope Saint, *Gaudete in Domino, On Christian Joy* (apostolic exhortation, May 9, 1975; online version)

(JN) Pelphrey, Brent, *Julian of Norwich: Christ, Our Mother* (Collegeville, MN: Liturgical Press [Michael Glazier Books], 1989)

(EDK) Philippe, Father Jacques, *The Eight Doors of the Kingdom: Meditations on the Beatitudes* (N.Y.: Scepter Publications, Inc., 2018)

RB) *RB 1980: The Rule of St. Benedict: In Latin and English with Notes*, edited by Timothy Fry, O.S.B. (Collegeville, MN: Liturgical Press, 1981)

(NS) Schellenberger, Fr. Bernardin, O.S.C.O., *Nomad of the Spirit* (N.Y.: The Crossroad Publishing Company, 1981)

(TS) Teresa of Calcutta, Saint, *Total Surrender*, ed. by Br. Angelo Demnanda (Ann Arbor, MI: Servant Publications, 1985)

(WS) Underhill, Evelyn, *The Ways of the Spirit*, ed. by Grace Adolphsen Brane (New York: The Crossroad Publishing Company, 1990)

ACKNOWLEDGMENTS

I would like to acknowledge with gratitude all those who, over the course of my life, have helped me to understand and to practice Christian joy. I thank my parents and childhood teachers who instilled in me a spirit of sacrifice of lesser goods for the sake of greater goods, though they may never have referred to "joy" as a fruit of healthy sacrifice. I thank my monastic formators and fellow monks who have found true joy in living by the *Rule* of St. Benedict, in making the monastic life more joyful for others, and in anticipating the fullness of joy in eternity. (Some of our younger monks speak about the goal of ultimate holiness and eternal life in Christ with amazing frequency.) I am grateful to Archabbot Paul Maher (now deceased), Archabbot Douglas Nowicki, and Archabbot Martin de Porres Bartel for appointing me as Director of Oblates and thus giving me opportunities to ponder more deeply the virtues of the *Rule*, to articulate them to our Oblates of St. Benedict, and to learn from many of our Oblates how to nurture joy in the Lord, even amid great trials. Most especially, I would like to thank Fr. Kurt Belsole, my confrere in this community, whose dissertation, *Joy in Lent*, and whose presentations to Oblates have provided me with the inspiration to ponder the topic, the energy to jot down these reflections, and the desire to share them, with humility and joy, with Oblates and others who seek to grow in Christian joy. Finally and most importantly, I offer thanks and praise to God, the source of all true joy, and who, in Jesus Christ, who "for the sake of the joy that lay before Him endured the cross" (Heb 12:2). May we all find our joy in "keeping our eyes fixed on Jesus, the leader and perfecter of faith" (Heb 12:2)!

Made in the USA
Middletown, DE
14 October 2022

12744402R00090